MAKE YOUR OWN

HORSE

CLOTHING

by
JEAN PERRY

Illustrated by
WILLIAM PERRY

J. A. ALLEN
London

By the same author

Make Your Own Horse Equipment

First published 1983
Reprinted 1984
Reprinted 1986
Reprinted 1988 (Twice)

Published by
J. A. Allen & Company Limited
1 Lower Grosvenor Place, Buckingham Palace Road,
London SW1W 0EL

© Jean Perry, 1983

British Library Cataloguing in Publication Data
Perry, Jean
Make your own horse clothing.
1. Horses—Clothing
I. Title
636.1'0837   SF285
ISBN 0-85131-383-3

Printed and bound in Great Britain

CONTENTS

	Introduction	1
1	Saddle cloths and numnahs:	2
	Shaped or square saddle cloth	2
	Bound numnah	7
	Unbound numnah	11
2	Saddle carrying bag	14
3	Applying bindings	19
4	Rugs and sheets:	23
	To make a pattern	23
	Applying straps and buckles	27
	Fillet string loops	33
	Surcingle loop	33
	Materials	34
	Day rug	36
	Anti-sweat rug	39
	Summer sheet	40
	Exercise sheet	42
	Unbound absorbent or lining rug	44
	Lined rug	47
	Foal rug	53
5	Surcingles	56
6	Fillet strings	58
7	Tail guard	65
8	Poll guard	70
9	Bandages	74
10	Yorkshire boots	78
11	Brushing boots	81
12	Travelling boots	85
13	Knee boots	91
14	Hock boots:	97
	Style A	97
	Style B	103
15	Coloured Brow band	106

INTRODUCTION

At a time when horse-owning is becoming more and more popular, many horses and ponies are being kept on a very tight budget. Naturally, most of the available cash goes on feed, bedding and health requirements, leaving little, if any, for rugs and other clothing. If you can use a sewing machine, you can make your own at a fraction of the ready-made cost.

Some of the items in this book can be made using materials which you may already have, but the finished article will only be as good as the materials from which you make it - a faded, moth-eaten blanket will not end up as a smart day rug. Markets are usually the best source of bought materials.

White or light-coloured wool blankets and cotton tapes, bindings and sheets can be dyed to almost any colour using the wash and dye method, so that items can be made to match in your own choice of colours. Materials made from synthetic fibres will often not accept dye at all, or, if they do, reduced colours may result. Instead of the deep rich red you intended, the end product is a delicate baby pink.

No special paper is required to convert the patterns to full size, newspaper is quite adequate. This can be stuck together with sticky tape to make larger sheets if one page is too small. However, if you intend to use a pattern several times, brown parcel wrapping paper will survive longer. To scale up the patterns, use a black felt-tipped pen, which will show up even on newspaper. Draw a grid of squares according to the scale shown for each item, and then copy on to it the shapes of the pattern pieces.

It should be possible to adapt the patterns to fit almost any size and shape of animal. If there is any doubt as to whether or not an item will fit your horse properly, it is a good idea to cut the pattern pieces out of odd scraps of material, tack them together and try on your horse or pony. Any adjustments can then be made before wasting your valuable time and materials.

There is no pattern for a New Zealand rug, and, although one of the rug patterns could be used for this, it would not be adviseable to attempt it. Apart from suitable waterproof materials being difficult to obtain and work with, incorrectly attached or unsuitable methods of securing the rug could prove dangerous.

With the exception of saddle sizes, all measurements are given in both imperial and metric units. All metric equivalents are approximate.

A seam allowance of $\frac{1}{2}$ inch (1.25 cm.) has been allowed throughout, unless otherwise stated.

1

CHAPTER 1

SADDLE CLOTHS AND NUMNAHS

A saddle cloth is made from one thickness of material, without padding, and helps to keep the underside of the saddle clean. Square saddle cloths sometimes have the owner's initials on the part of the cloth which shows behind the rider's leg.

A numnah is a pad which helps to reduce pressure on a horse's back. Fabric numnahs are made from two thicknesses of material with foam between; the thickness of the foam determines the thickness of the numnah.

When you fit a saddle cloth or numnah to your saddle, remember to make sure that it is smooth under the saddle, and that you pull the centre seam up into the gullet so that it does not press on your horse's back. If it does press, it could cause galls and eventually patches of white hair.

SHAPED OR SQUARE SADDLE CLOTH

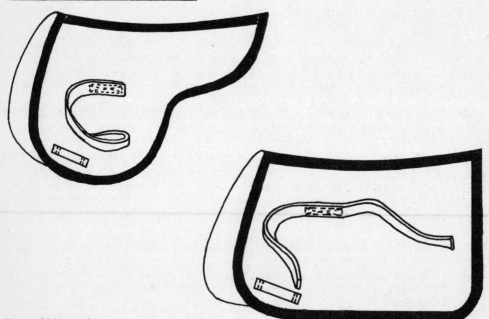

You will need:

1¼ yards (1.25 m.) of 35/36 inch (90 cm.) wide cotton or blanket-weight material.

5½ yards (5 m.) of 1 inch (2.5 cm.) wide tape or braid for binding.

Sewing thread to match the binding.

To make

1. Fold the material in half across the width and cut out one pair of the shapes shown for the type of saddle cloth chosen.

PATTERN 1   -   SQUARE SADDLE CLOTH

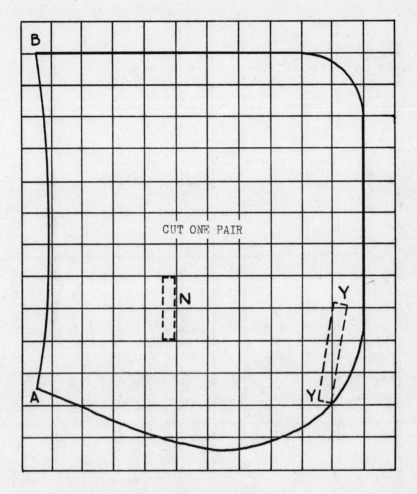

EACH SQUARE REPRESENTS 2 INCHES (5 CM.)
CUT AROUND SOLID LINE ONLY.
The pattern given is for a 17 inch G.P. saddle.

For a 16 inch saddle, trim ½ inch (1.25 cm.) off the pattern all
the way round.

For a 15 inch saddle, trim 1 inch (2.5 cm.) off the pattern all
the way round.

For an 18 inch saddle, add ½ inch (1.25 cm.) to the pattern all
the way round.

PATTERN 2   -   SHAPED SADDLE CLOTH

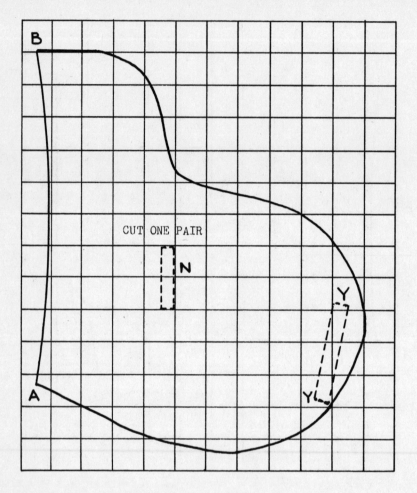

EACH SQUARE REPRESENTS 2 INCHES (5 CM.)
CUT AROUND SOLID LINE ONLY.
The pattern is for a 17 inch G.P. saddle.

For a 16 inch saddle, trim ½ inch (1.25 cm.) off the pattern all
the way round.

For a 15 inch saddle, trim 1 inch (2.5 cm.) off the pattern all
the way round.

For an 18 inch saddle, add ½ inch (1.25 cm.) to the pattern all
the way round.

2. With the wrong sides of the material together, join the two pieces together along the top line AB.

3. Press the seam to one side using a warm iron, and stitch the seam flat. (Fig. 1)

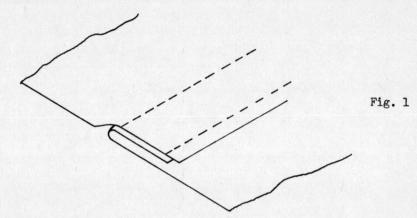

Fig. 1

4. Cut a piece of tape or braid to the same length as the seam. Cover the seam with the binding by stitching along it close to each edge. (Fig. 2)

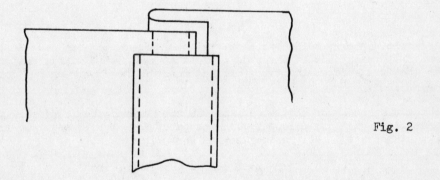

Fig. 2

5. Bind the edge of the saddle cloth using Method B described in Chapter 3.

6. Cut two pieces of binding each 7 inches (18 cm.) long. Fold under 1 inch (2.5 cm.) at each end, and stitch the pieces of binding at the positions shown (Y to Y) on the pattern to form keepers for the girth. (Fig. 3)

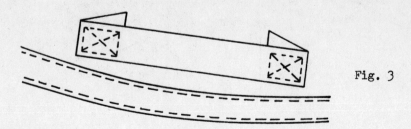

Fig. 3

7. Cut the remaining piece of tape or braid in half and find the middle of each piece. Sew one piece of tape on to each side of the saddle cloth at position N on the pattern so that the free ends are approximately the same length. (Fig. 4)

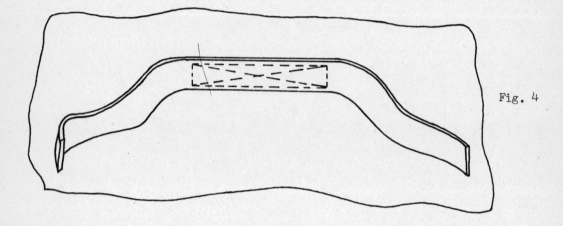

Fig. 4

Tie these tapes around your saddle panels to keep the saddle cloth in place.

Or:

8. Cut the remaining piece of tape or braid in half. Sew one end of each piece on to each side of the saddle cloth at position N on the pattern, with the free ends of the tape pointing towards the front edge of the saddle cloth.

9. Try the cloth on your saddle. Pass the tape around the front edge of the saddle panel, and pin a loop in each piece of tape to fit securely around the girth straps. Stitch the loop as shown in Fig. 5.

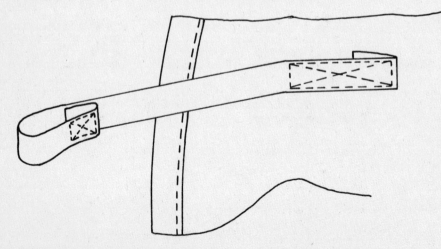

Fig. 5

BOUND NUMNAH

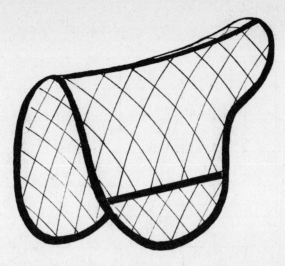

The instructions are for a numnah with pockets for the saddle panels. Thin foam should be used for the filling so that the binding can be applied easily and the pocket does not make the lower edge of the numnah too bulky. It is not suitable for a saddle with half panels, for which a girth loop fixing, as described for the saddle cloth, should be used.

You could make it with a panel loop instead for a full panel saddle, as described for the unbound numnah, in which case you can use thicker foam, although it will then be difficult to apply the binding.

You should allow an extra 1 yard (1 m.) of binding for girth loops.

If the numnah is made with girth loops or a panel loop, leave out steps 8 to 11.

For a quilted numnah, either use ready-quilted material or quilt it yourself after steps 6 and 9, by machining rows of stitching in two directions through all layers of the work. (NOTE: QUILTED NYLON ANORAK MATERIAL IS NOT SUITABLE).

You will need:

3 yards (2.75 m.) of 35/36 inch (90 cm.) wide material.

Or 1½ yards (1.5 m.) of 54 inch (140 cm.) wide material.

2 pieces of thin foam, each 26 inches (66 cm.) x 22 inches (56 cm.)

5 yards (4.5 m.) of 1½ inch (4 cm.) wide tape or braid for binding.

Sewing thread to match the binding.

To Make

1. Fold 54 inch (140 cm.) wide material in half across the width.
   Fold 36 inch (90 cm.) wide material in four across the width.
   Cut out 2 pairs of the shapes shown in material and 1 pair in foam.
   (Save the pieces of material and foam left over for the panel pocket).

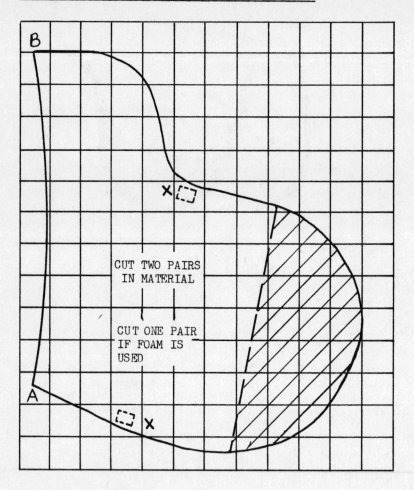

For a BOUND NUMNAH cut out the pattern as shown.

For an UNBOUND NUMNAH, add ½ inch (1.25 cm.) seam allowance all the way round.

EACH SQUARE REPRESENTS 2 INCHES (5 CM.)
CUT AROUND SOLID LINE ONLY.
The pattern is for a 17 inch G.P. saddle.

For a 16 inch saddle, trim ½ inch (1.25 cm.) off the pattern all the way round.

For a 15 inch saddle, trim 1 inch (2.5 cm.) off the pattern all the way round.

For an 18 inch saddle, add ½ inch (1.25 cm.) to the pattern all the way round.

2. With the right sides of the material together, sew one pair of material
   shapes together along the top line AB for the upper side of your numnah,
   and one pair for the underside. (Fig. 6)

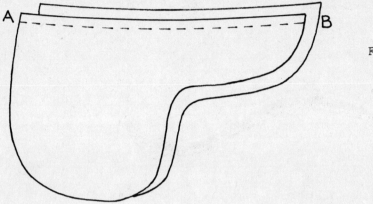

Fig. 6

3. Using a warm iron, press the seams open.

4. Overlap the top edges (AB) of the two pieces of foam and tack them
   together. (Fig. 7)

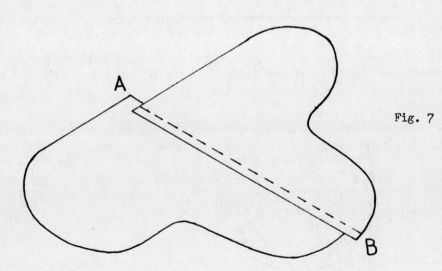

Fig. 7

5. Place the foam between the two joined pieces of work (with their right sides to the outside). Stitch through the three layers along the line AB. (Fig. 8).

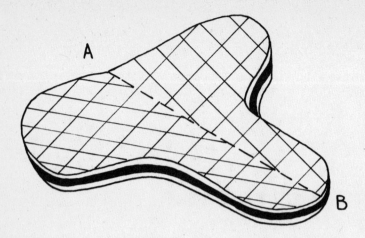

Fig. 8

6. Stitch through all three layers all the way round, close to the edge.

7. Decide which is to be the upper side of the numnah. Cut a piece of tape long enough to cover the seam AB and stitch this down along both edges of the tape on the upper side of the numnah.

8. Take the pieces of material and foam you have left over from cutting out the numnah. Cut out 2 pairs of material and 1 pair of foam shapes to the shape of the shaded part of the pattern.

9. With the wrong sides of the material together, place a piece of foam between each pair of shapes and stitch through all three layers all the way round, close to the edge.

10. Cut a piece of binding long enough to bind the straight edge of each of these two shapes. Bind the straight edge using Method A described in Chapter 3.

11. Place the bound pieces on the upper side of the numnah at the lower edge of the saddle flap (the shaded portion of the pattern). Stitch the pieces in place around the unbound edge. (Fig. 9)

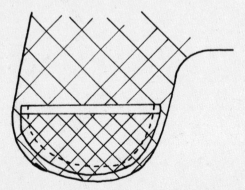

Fig. 9

12. Starting at the centre back seam, bind the numnah right round the edge using method A.

UNBOUND NUMNAH

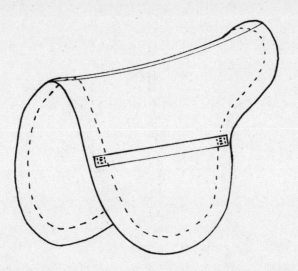

The instructions are for a numnah with a panel loop fixing. It is not suitable for a half panel saddle, for which a girth loop fixing should be used as described for the saddle cloth. Allow an extra 1 yard (1 m.) of binding for girth loops.

You will need:

2½ yards (2.5 m.) of 35/36 inch (90 cm.) wide material.

Or 1½ yards (1.5 m.) of 54 inch (140 cm.) wide material.

2 pieces of foam each 26 inches (66 cm.) x 22 inches (56 cm.) x 1 inch (2.5 cm.)

1 yard (1 m.) of 1 inch (2.5 cm.) wide tape or webbing.

To Make

1. Fold 54 inch (140 cm.) wide material in half across the width.
   Fold 36 inch (90 cm.) wide material in four across the width.
   Cut out 2 pairs of the shapes shown in material and 1 pair in foam.

2. Take one pair of the shapes in material for the upper side of the numnah.
   With the right sides of the material together, join these along the top line AB.

3. Take the other pair of shapes for the under side of the numnah. With the right sides of the material together, join 3 inches (7.5 cm.) along the top line from point A, and 3 inches (7.5 cm.) along the top line from point B. Leave the centre portion of the seam open. (Fig. 10)

11

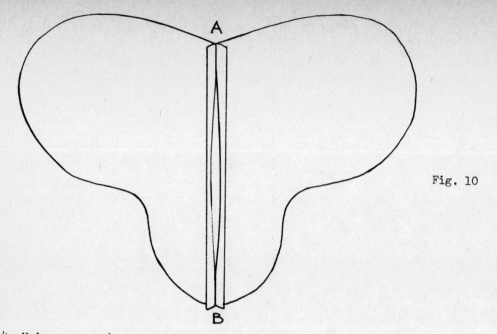

Fig. 10

4. Using a warm iron, press the seams open.

5. Place the right sides of the two joined pieces together, and stitch them together all the way round the edge.

6. Press the seam open and turn the work through to the right side, through the opening in the centre top line.

7. Fit one piece of foam into each side of the numnah through the open seam. Overlap the edges AB of the foam.

8. Close the centre seam by oversewing it manually.

9. Stitch through both layers of material and the foam ½ inch (1.25 cm.) each side of the centre seam. (Fig. 11)
   (Note: The numnah should compress sufficiently to fit under the foot of your sewing machine, but, if it does not, it will be necessary to keep the foot in the raised position and ease the work through).

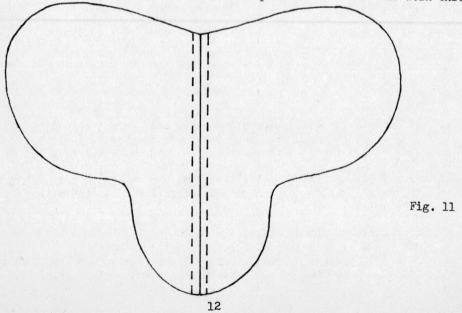

Fig. 11

12

10. Stitch through the 3 layers of the numnah all the way round, 2½ to 3 inches (6.25 cm. to 7.5 cm.) in from the edge. (Fig. 12)

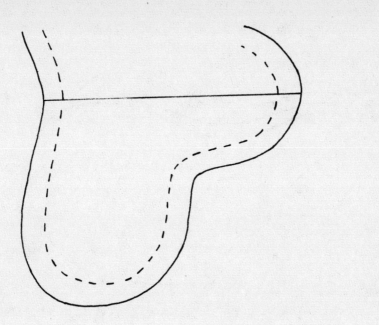

Fig. 12

11. Measure the distance X to X indicated on the pattern, add an inch and cut a piece of tape to that length. Fold under ½ inch (1.25 cm.) at each end and stitch the ends down through the 3 layers. (Fig. 13)

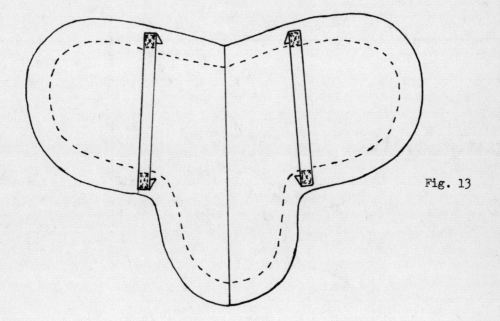

Fig. 13

CHAPTER 2

GENERAL PURPOSE SADDLE CARRYING BAG

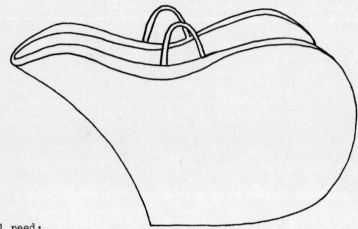

You will need:

2¼ yards (2 m.) of 35/36 inch (90 cm.) wide material.
A 36 inch (90 cm.) zip.

To make

1. Fold the material in half across the width and, using the layout shown in
   Fig. 14, cut out 2 pairs of the saddle shapes. Cut out 2 strips of material
   each 2 inches (5 cm.) wide by 12 inches (20 cm.) long for the handles.

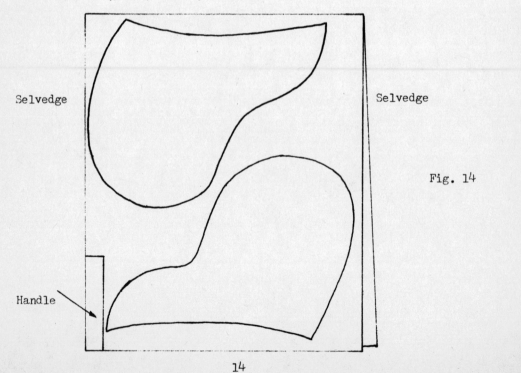

Selvedge

Selvedge

Fig. 14

Handle

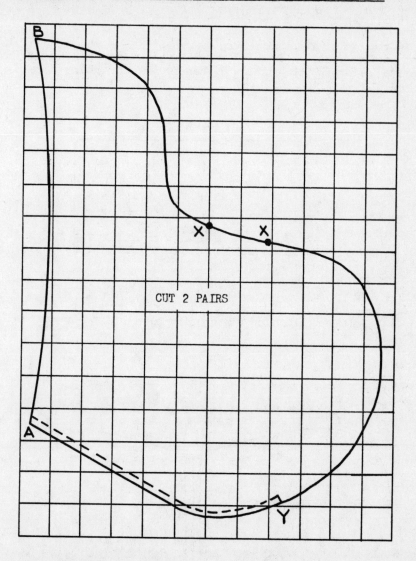

EACH SQUARE REPRESENTS 2 INCHES (5 CM.)
CUT AROUND SOLID LINE ONLY
The pattern is for a 17 inch General Purpose saddle.

For a 16 inch saddle, trim ½ inch (1.25 cm.) off the pattern all
the way round.

For a 15 inch saddle, trim 1 inch (2.5 cm.) off the pattern all
the way round.

For an 18 inch saddle, add ½ inch (1.25 cm.) to the pattern all
the way round.

2. With the right sides of the material together, join one pair of the shapes along the top line AB to cover the upper side of your saddle, and one pair to cover the underside. Neaten the edges of the seams, and press the seams open using a warm iron. (Seam neatening methods are shown at the end of this chapter).

3. Fold the two handle strips lengthways and sew as shown in Fig. 15. Press the handles flat. (This method will give a stronger handle than if the strips were sewn into tubes and then turned through).

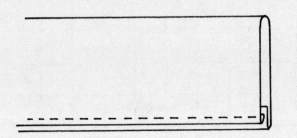

Fig. 15

4. Place the two joined pieces with right sides together, and pin the handles at the positions indicated on the pattern so that they are inside the bag. (Fig. 16)

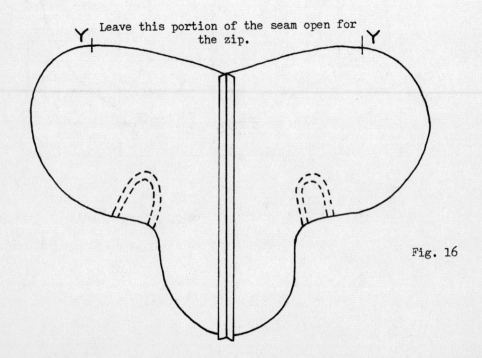

Leave this portion of the seam open for the zip.

Fig. 16

5. Tack round the edge from Y to Y, securing the handles in position, and leaving the front edge open for the zip. (Place the zip along the front edge of the bag to decide where points Y should be).

6. Machine stitch around the outside from Y to Y. Remove the tacking stitches and neaten the raw edges, including the unjoined edges where the zip will go.

7. Press the seam open. Fold the seam allowance along the unjoined zip edges to the wrong side and press these folds in place.

8. Turn the bag through to the right side and insert the zip (Fig. 17). (Note: On garments, zips are hidden in seams to give a neat appearance. This is not necessary with a saddle bag. Also, leaving the zip exposed avoids material being caught in it when the bag is being zipped up or unzipped).

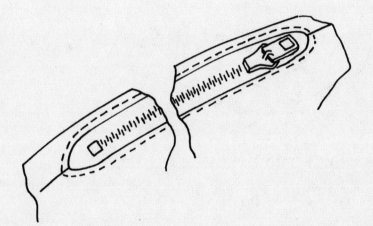

Fig. 17

To Neaten Seams

The following methods of neatening seams are quick and easy, but you could use any other method you prefer.

1. Zig-zag machine stitch along each of the raw edges of the seam. (Fig. 18)

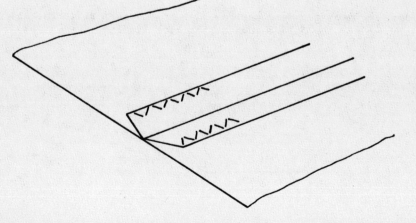

Fig. 18

17

2. Fold the raw edges under and zig-zag machine stitch along the folded edge. (Fig. 19)

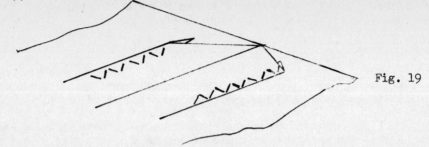

Fig. 19

3. Fold the raw edges under and straight machine stitch along the folded edge. (Fig. 20)

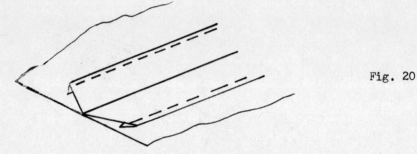

Fig. 20

4. Bind the raw edges with bias binding as follows:-

   (a) Unfold one edge of the bias binding, and straight machine stitch this to the underside of the seam. (Fig. 21)

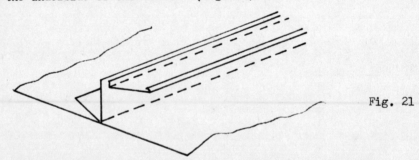

Fig. 21

   (b) Wrap the binding around the raw edge of the seam and straight machine stitch along the folded edge of the bias binding. (Fig. 22)

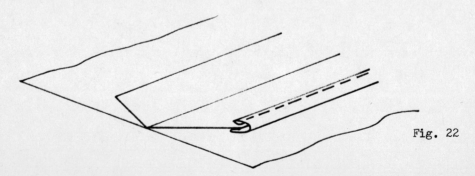

Fig. 22

CHAPTER 3

APPLYING BINDINGS

METHOD A is suitable for a bound numnah, knee boots, a day rug or an exercise sheet with 1½ inch (4 cm.) wide binding.

For rugs and numnahs start the binding at the centre back seam.

If you are not sure whether you can stitch the binding on neatly after just pinning it in place, tack it in position first.

Stitch the binding to the right side of the material so that approximately one third of the width of the binding protrudes beyond the edge of the work. (Fig. 23)

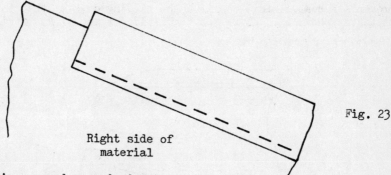

Fig. 23

Right side of
material

Ease the binding around curved edges.

At corners, fold the binding as shown in Fig. 24 to give a mitred effect. Stitch along the fold from the edge of the binding, up to the corner, and back to the edge of the binding again.

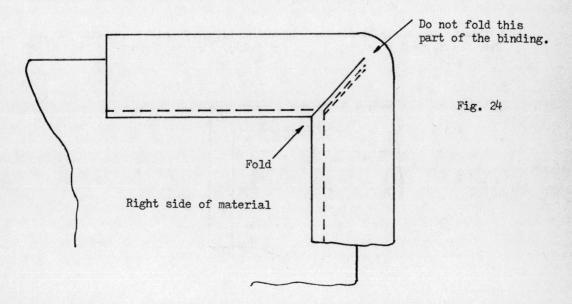

Do not fold this
part of the binding.

Fig. 24

Fold

Right side of material

When you reach the place where the binding was started, finish off by folding the end of the binding under and stitching across the fold as shown in Fig. 25.

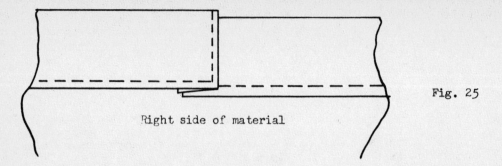

Right side of material

Fig. 25

Turn the work over, and fold the binding around the edge of the material. Tack the binding in place on this side and trim off any material which prevents a neat finish.   Stitch the binding down so that this row of stitching shows through on the right side of the work.   (Fig. 26)

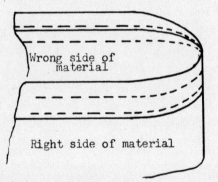

Wrong side of material

Right side of material

Fig. 26

Ease the binding around curved edges.

At corners, fold the binding as shown in Fig. 27 to give a mitred effect. (There is no need to stitch along the folded edge at corners on this side of the work).

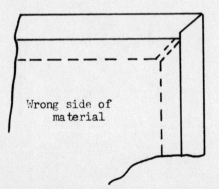

Wrong side of material

Fig. 27

METHOD B is suitable for saddle cloths, a summer sheet, or an exercise sheet with 1 inch (2.5 cm.) wide binding.

Fold approximately ½ inch (1.25 cm.) of the edge to be bound to the right side of the work all the way round the sheet or cloth, and press down using a warm iron.   (Fig. 27)

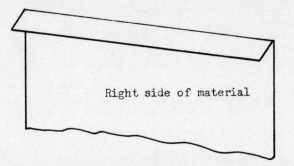

Right side of material

Fig. 27

Start the binding at the centre back seam, and place the binding on the right side of the work, so that the edge of the binding just overlaps the folded edge.   Tack the binding in place through the folded material. (Fig. 28)

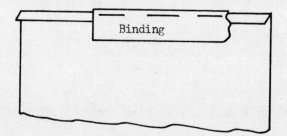

Binding

Fig. 28

Ease the binding around curved edges.

At corners, fold the binding to give a mitred effect. (Fig. 29)

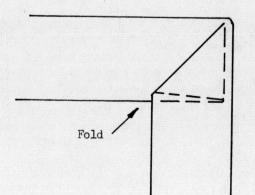

Fold

Fig. 29

When you reach the place where the binding was started, finish off by folding the end of the binding under as shown in Fig. 30.

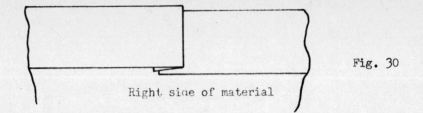

Right side of material

Fig. 30

Using thread to match the binding, stitch the outer edge of the binding in place from the wrong side of the work close to the folded edge of the material. (Fig. 31)

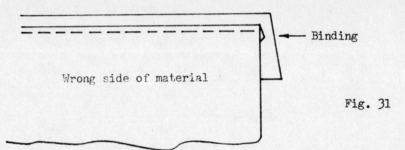

Wrong side of material

← Binding

Fig. 31

Stitch along the inner edge of the binding from the right side of the work.

At corners, stitch along the folded edge of the binding and back again. (Fig. 32)

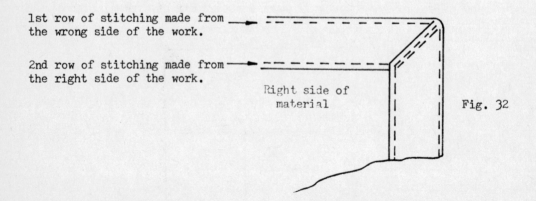

1st row of stitching made from the wrong side of the work.

2nd row of stitching made from the right side of the work.

Right side of material

Fig. 32

When you reach the place where the binding is joined (at the centre back seam), stitch across the join.

22

CHAPTER 4

RUGS AND SHEETS

TO MAKE A RUG PATTERN

If you are fortunate enough to have a "rug-shaped horse" and already have a rug which fits, (or can borrow one from a friend), use this to make a pattern. If you do not, proceed as follows:

1. Make measurements A to G as shown in Fig. 33.

   It may be helpful in making measurements E, F and G to chalk lines E and F, and the position of the rug neckline, on your horse.

   Make sure that the neckline is high enough - the rug should cover your horse's shoulder blade. If it hangs below the shoulder blade, it is likely to rub bald patches in your horse's coat.

2. Transfer measurements A and B to a piece of paper of sufficient size. (Sheets of newspaper stuck together with sticky tape will do). Cut out the rectangle formed by these measurements.

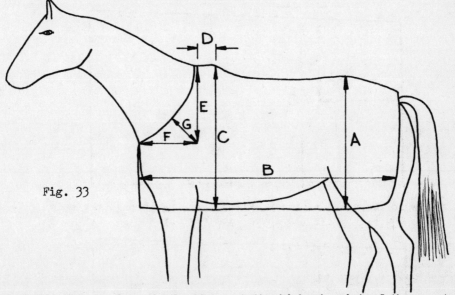

Fig. 33

A - Depth of the rug from the backbone at the highest point of the quarters.

B - Length of the rug from the back edge to the centre of the chest.

C - Depth of the rug from the highest point of the withers.

D - Distance from the point of the withers to the edge of the rug neckline.

E - Distance from the top of the neckline to a point in line with the front of the neckline.

F - Distance from the front of the neckline to line E.

G - Distance from the point where lines E and F meet to the edge of the neckline (bisecting the angle made by lines E and F).

3. Mark the position of line C (distance F plus distance D from the front edge). Starting at the bottom edge of the pattern, draw in line C.

4. Draw a line starting at the top back corner (point Y) through the top line C, to touch the front edge at point X. (Fig. 34)

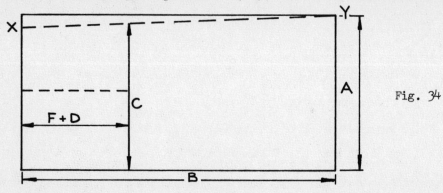

Fig. 34

5. Starting at line XY, draw in line E, distance D from line C.   Starting at the front edge, draw in line F to meet line E.

From the point where lines E and F meet, bisect the angle made by lines E and F with line G.   (Fig. 35)

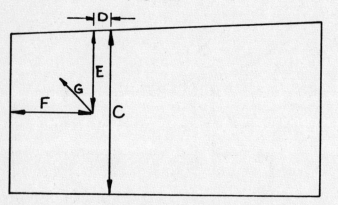

Fig. 35

6. Draw in the shape of the neckline, passing through the ends of lines E, G and F.   Curve the lower back edge as shown.   (Fig. 36)

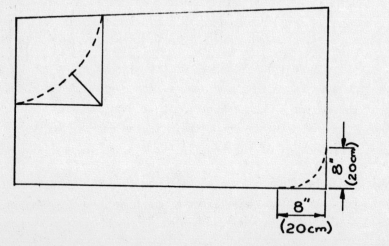

Fig. 36

8" (20cm)

8" (20cm)

24

7. Mark the position of the fillet string loops 12 inches (30 cm.) from the back edge and 15 inches (38 cm.) from the lower edge as shown in Fig. 37.

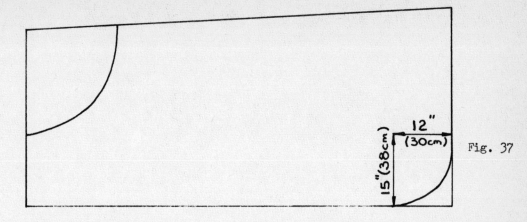

15"(38cm)   12" (30cm)

Fig. 37

8. The centre top seam shaping cannot be decided until you try the cut out rug on your horse.

When you have cut the rug out according to the pattern you have made, with the wrong sides of the material together, pin the top seam together. Try the rug shape on your horse and carefully rearrange the pins to give the top seam shaping. Cut the top seam to the shape made by the pins, allowing ½ inch (1.25 cm.) extra for the seam allowance. Transfer this shaping to your pattern for future use.

NOTE: BE VERY CAREFUL WITH THE PINS WHEN TRYING THE RUG MATERIAL ON YOUR HORSE. YOU SHOULD PIN THEM SECURELY INTO THE MATERIAL, AND DO THIS IN A PLACE WHERE, IF YOU DROP ANY PINS, THEY CAN BE EASILY SEEN. GLASS HEADED PINS ARE BEST, AS THEY ARE LONGER AND MORE EASILY SEEN IF DROPPED.

9. You can add additional shaping to your rug to give it a better fit.

Put darts in the neck if your horse has rounded shoulders to make it fit snugly.
Put darts at the lower and/or back edges if he has very rounded quarters. (Fig. 38)

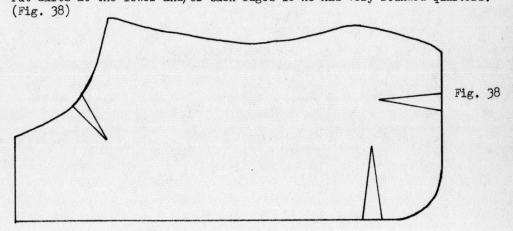

Fig. 38

Darts should be on the outside of a rug to avoid points of pressure.

Fit the rug on your horse after joining the centre top seam, and carefully pin the darts in position.

After sewing the dart, stitch it flat before binding the edge of the rug. (Fig. 39)

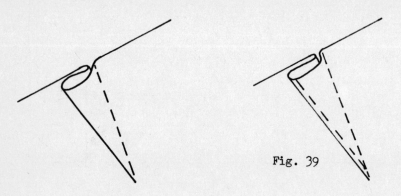

Fig. 39

If you are making a lined rug, darts should not be sewn into the lining.

Put small folds into the lining material near the dart, but not level with it. This will spread the thickness of the material.   (Fig. 40)

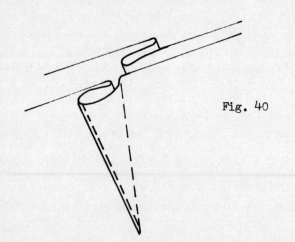

Fig. 40

APPLYING STRAPS AND BUCKLES

Types of buckle

Rocco (pinless) for use on both
rugs and surcingles.

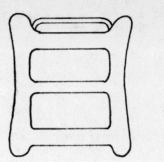

Single roller - best used on
surcingles.

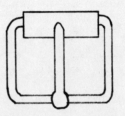

Fig. 41

Double roller - best used on
rugs.

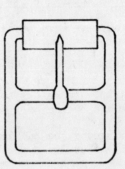

You may be able to buy straps and buckles from an obliging saddler or you
can salvage them from items no longer in use.

Nylon webbing for straps can be purchased from shops specialising in outdoor
pursuits.

Straps and buckles should be approximately 1 inch (2.5 cm.) wide.

Secondhand sources of buckles and straps

Single and double roller buckles, and leather for straps can be salvaged from
old leather head collars.

Double roller and rocco buckles, and nylon webbing for straps can be saved
from old nylon head collars.

Save buckles and straps from discarded rugs, rollers and surcingles.

Other suitable buckles and leather for straps can be obtained from old
stirrup leathers.

NOTE: Dress buckles are not suitable as they are not strong enough.

To attach leather straps and buckles

If the straps you are using do not already have stitch holes punched in them, a leather awl must be used to make them. You should be able to buy one, quite cheaply, from a handicraft shop, saddler or other shop dealing in leatherwork.

Mark the position of the stitches with a sharply pointed dressmaker's tracing wheel.

A harness or plaiting needle is the most satisfactory for use in this type of work, and you can buy one from your local tack shop.

Linen thread (button thread) should be drawn through a block of beeswax before use. Any shop selling dressmaking materials should sell these.

You will probably find that the easiest way to sew leather straps to your rug is to use back stitch.

To attach nylon webbing straps and buckles

You can attach these to your rug by machine stitching, and you will not have to mark or punch stitch holes.

Seal cut edges of nylon webbing by passing the edge carefully through a flame.

To attach a pinless buckle to its straps

Cut a piece of nylon webbing or leather 6 inches (15 cm.) long and the correct width to fit through the buckle you are using.

Fold the leather or webbing in half over the centre bar of the buckle.

For a leather strap, use an awl to make two holes through both layers of leather close to the buckle bar. For nylon webbing, no holes are made.

Secure the strap around the buckle by stitching several times through the two layers as shown. (For leather, use the two holes you have just made). (Fig. 42)

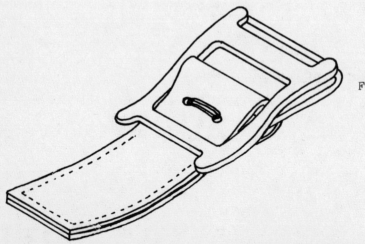

Fig. 42

To attach a buckle with a pin to its strap

Cut a piece of leather or nylon webbing 6 inches (15 cm.) long and the correct width to fit through the buckle.

Mark the centre of the strap.

For a leather strap use a leather punch to make two holes 1 inch (2.5 cm.) apart. Using a modelling knife, cut out the strip of leather between the holes as shown. (Fig. 43)

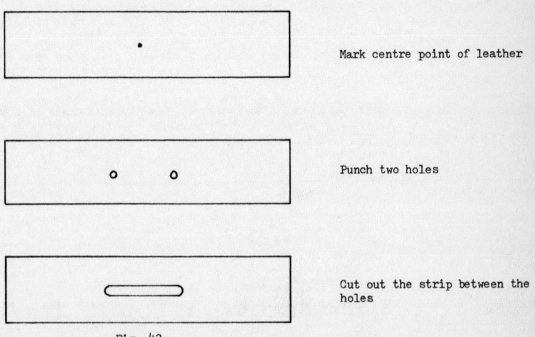

Mark centre point of leather

Punch two holes

Cut out the strip between the holes

Fig. 43

For a nylon webbing strap burn out the holes and slot using a steel knitting needle or a nail which has been heated. HOLD THE KNITTING NEEDLE OR NAIL IN A PAIR OF PLIERS SO THAT YOU DO NOT BURN YOURSELF.

For both types of strap, slot the strap over the pin of the buckle and secure it around the buckle by stitching through the two layers of the strap as described for the pinless buckle. (Fig. 44)

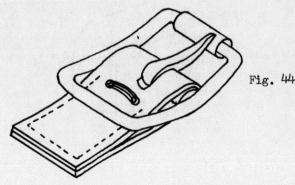

Fig. 44

Applying straps and buckles to rugs

Cut a strap 8 inches (20 cm.) long to partner the one you have already fitted to a buckle.

Cut one end into a point. Using an awl, make stitch holes for about 2 inches (5 cm.) along the other end of a leather strap. (Fig. 45)

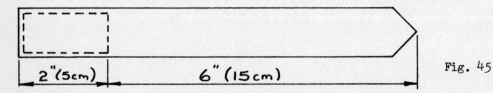

Fig. 45

If your buckle has a pin, make holes in this strap approximately 1 inch (2.5 cm.) apart. Use a leather punch for a leather strap and a heated knitting needle or nail for a nylon strap.

Place the strap with the buckle on the rug far enough in from the edge that the buckle does not reach the edge of the rug. It should be approximately 2 inches (5 cm.) down from the neck edge so that it does not restrict the movement of your horse's neck. (Fig. 46)

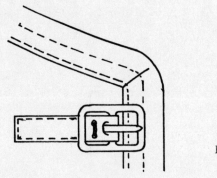

Fig. 46

For leather, stitch along one side of the strap, across the end and back along the other side. (Fig. 46)

If you are using nylon webbing, stitch all the way round and across the centre as shown. (Fig. 47)

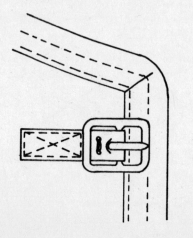

Fig. 47

Attach a corresponding strap to the other side of the rug, the same distance down from the neck edge so that the edge of the stitched end of the strap is about 3 inches (8 cm.) in from the front edge of the rug.   Stitch the end 2 inches (5 cm.) of the strap to the rug.   (Fig. 48)

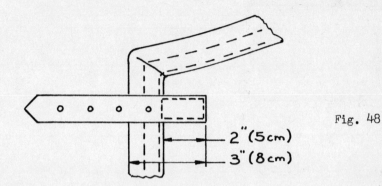

Fig. 48

For nylon webbing, stitch across the centre of the stitched end as you did for the strap with the buckle.

To attach straps and buckles to surcingles

Cut a strap 14 inches (36 cm.) long.   Cut one end to a point.   If you are using leather, punch stitch holes in the other end with an awl.

If your buckle has a pin, make holes in this strap approximately 1 inch (2.5 cm.) apart, using a leather punch for a leather strap or a heated knitting needle or nail for a nylon strap.

Attach the buckle to a strap as previously described.

Fold both ends of the surcingle as shown in Fig. 49.

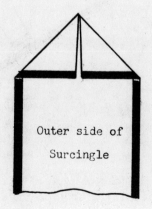

Outer side of
Surcingle

Fig. 49

31

Place the strap without the buckle over the folded in edges at one end, and stitch the strap in place.   (Fig. 50)

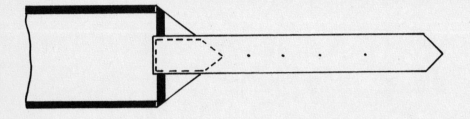

Fig. 50

For a nylon webbing strap, stitch across the centre of the stitched end as previously described.

Place the buckle straps over the other end of the surcingle as shown in Fig. 51, and stitch in place in the same way as the first strap.

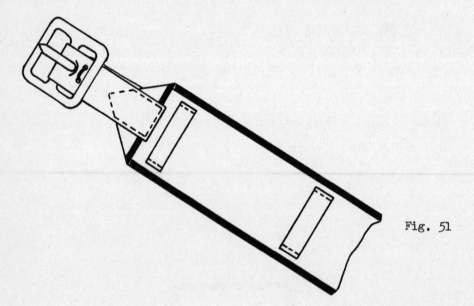

Fig. 51

Stitch a keeper, made from a strip of leather or nylon webbing, across the outer side of the surcingle at the buckle end, approximately 4 inches (10 cm.) from the buckle.   Stitch another keeper 5 inches (12.5 cm.) from the first. (Fig. 51)

To attach fillet string loops to a rug

Cut two pieces of binding each 6 inches (15 cm.) long.

If you are using 1½ inch (4 cm.) wide binding, fold it in half down the length. For 1 inch (2.5 cm.) wide binding, do not fold it.

Now fold the binding into three as shown in Fig. 52.

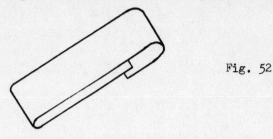

Fig. 52

Stitch one piece to the inside of the rug at the position indicated on the pattern, using thread to match the rug.   (Fig. 53)   (The loop should point towards the curved lower back edge).

Fig. 53

Stitch the other pieces at the same position on the other side of the rug.

To attach a surcingle loop to a rug

When the rug is finished, try it on your horse.   Mark the position of the surcingle on the centre top seam binding.   (A felt-tipped or ball-point pen will do).

Cut a piece of binding 3½ inches (9 cm.) longer than the width of the surcingle.

Turn under ¼ inch (0.625 cm.) of the binding at each end, and stitch it in place as shown in Fig. 54, over the centre top seam binding.

Width of surcingle
+ 1 inch (2.5 cm.)

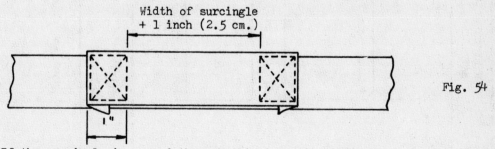

Fig. 54

If the surcingle is passed through this loop, it will help to prevent the rug sliding back in wear.

MATERIALS FOR RUGS

RUG	WIDTH OF MATERIAL	AMOUNT OF MATERIAL	EXTRA MATERIAL FOR SURCINGLE	AMOUNT OF BINDING	ACCESSORIES
Day rug Summer sheet Anti-sweat rug	35/36" (90 cm.)	2 x length	½ yd. (0.5 m.) for surcingle up to 6 ft. (180 cm.) + a further 1/8 yd. (0.125 m.) for surcingle over 6 ft. (180cm.)	For rug: (3 x length) + (4 x depth) + 1 yd. (1 m.)	(a) Strap and buckle for rug.
	45" (115 cm.)	2 x length	None if surcingle no longer than rug of maximum depth 36" (90 cm.) Rug deeper than 36" (90 cm.): + ½ yd. (0.5 m.) for surcingle up to 7'6" (226 cm.)		(b) Strap and buckle for surcingle
	54" (136 cm.)	2 x length	None	For surcingle: (2 x length) + ¼ yd. (25 cm.)	(c) Fillet string
	72" (180 cm.)	1 x length	¼ yd. (25 cm.) for surcingle up to 6 ft. (180 cm.) + a further 1/8 yd. (12.5 cm.) for surcingle over 6 ft.(180 cm.)		No surcingle or fillet string required for Anti-sweat rug.
	For Day rug only: 1 blanket 70" (180 cm.) x 90" (230 cm.)		None		
Unbound rug	As Day rug and Summer sheet	As Day rug and Summer sheet		(1 x length) + (2 x depth)	As Day rug and Summer sheet.
Lined rug	As Day rug for both top layer and lining material.		As Day rug - surcingle from top layer material only.	2 yrds. (2 m.) of 35/36" (90 cm.) nylon lining for rug. 3/4 yd.(0.75m.) for surcingle.	As Day rug and Summer sheet, but no fillet string.

RUG	WIDTH OF	AMOUNT OF MATERIAL	EXTRA MATERIAL FOR SURCINGLE	AMOUNT OF BINDING	ACCESSORIES
Foal rug	35/36" (90 cm.)	2 x length + 3/4 yard (0.75 m.)	Tail bandage with tapes removed or 1½ (4 cm.) wide tape measuring distance round girth ½ yd. (0.5 m.)	(1 x length) + ½ yd. (0.5 m.)	None
Exercise sheet	35/36" (90 cm.) and 45" (115 cm.)	2 x length	None	(3 x length) + (4 x depth)	Fillet string
	54" (136 cm.) to 72" (180 cm.)	1 x length			
1 Travelling rug					

You will need:

Blanket-weight material according to the material chart on page 34.
1½ inch (4 cm.) wide tape or braid for binding.
Sewing thread to match both the binding and the rug.
Straps and buckles.

To make

1. Cut out one pair of rug shapes.   From the piece of material cut out of
   the neck, cut 2 pieces each 5 inches (13 cm.) wide for reinforcement at
   the front neck edge. (Fig. 55)
   (If the remaining pieces from the neck are 10 inches (25 cm.) x 15 inches
   (38 cm.) long at the centre, they can be used to make a tail guard).

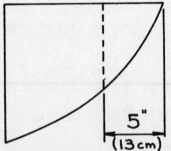

5"
(13 cm)

Fig. 55

2. With the wrong sides of the material together, join the centre top seam,
   using thread to match the binding.   Fold the seam to one side and stitch
   it down.   (Fig. 56)

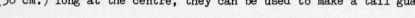

Fig. 56

3. Stitch two strips of binding, each with 3 rows of stitching as shown in
   Fig. 57.

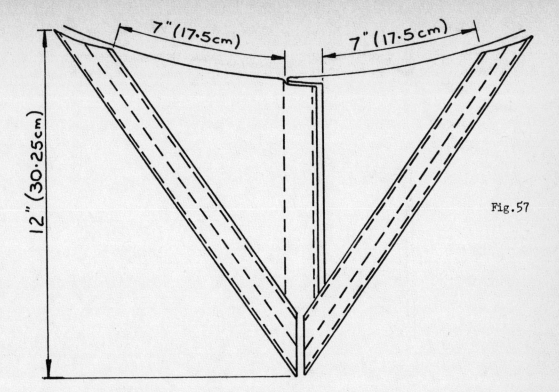

7" (17·5cm) 7" (17·5cm)

12" (30·25cm)

Fig. 57

4. Cover the centre top seam, by stitching a strip of binding along it, using 3 rows of stitching. (Fig. 58)

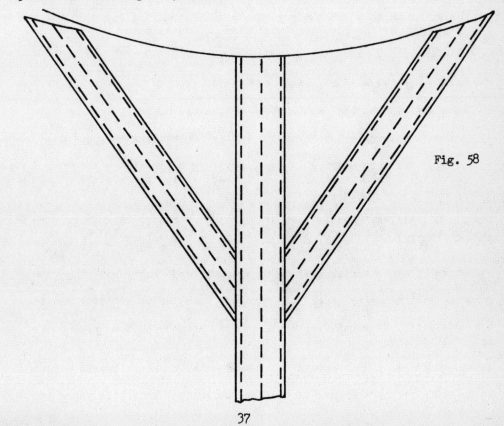

Fig. 58

5. On the wrong side of the material, using thread to match the rug, stitch the reinforcing pieces to the front neck edge. Put a row of stitching all around the curve of the neck of the rug to prevent it stretching when it is being bound. (Fig. 59)

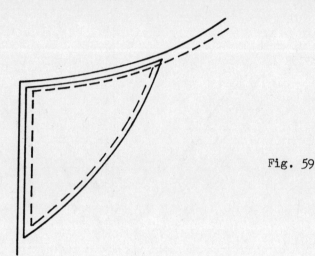

Fig. 59

6. Using thread to match the binding, start at the centre back edge, and bind round the rug using Method A as described in Chapter 3.

7. Using thread to match the rug, stitch fillet string loops on the inside of the rug at the positions indicated on the pattern.

8. Attach a strap and buckle.

9. Make a surcingle as described in Chapter 5.

10. Make a fillet string as described in Chapter 6.

11. Attach a surcingle loop over the centre top binding if required.

A day rug looks very smart with the owner's initials at the lower back edge. You can buy initials from tack shops in basic colours, or you can make your own in any colour you wish.

Bought initials are usually made of felt, which cannot be washed. So if you have made your rug from washable material, and you think that you may want to wash it, your initials will also need to be washable material.

Almost any plain material will do provided it does not fray.

Draw the letters on to graph paper and cut them out to use as templates.

Use a felt-tipped or ball-point pen to draw around the templates on the material to be used.

Stitch your initials on carefully by hand after tacking them in position, or, if you are efficient with a sewing machine, zig-zag stitch around them in thread which matches either the rug or the initial material.

ANTI-SWEAT RUG

By using appropriate material, the instructions for the day rug can be used
to make an anti-sweat rug.

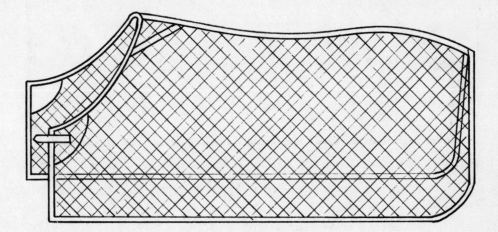

You will need:

Cotton mesh (string vest) material according to the material chart on page 34.

A piece of cotton material to match the cotton mesh 6 inches (15 cm.) x 12 inches
(30 cm.).

½ inch (1.25 cm.) wide seam tape for the centre top seam.

1½ inch (4 cm.) wide tape or braid for the centre top seam and for binding.

Sewing thread to match the binding.

Straps and buckle.

To make

1. Cut out one pair of rug shapes in cotton mesh and 2 pieces in material to
   reinforce the front neck edge.

2. Tack ½ inch (1.25 cm.) wide seam tape along the centre top seam to prevent
   it from stretching.

3. Carry out steps 2, 3, 4, 5, 6 and 8 as described for the day rug on page 36.

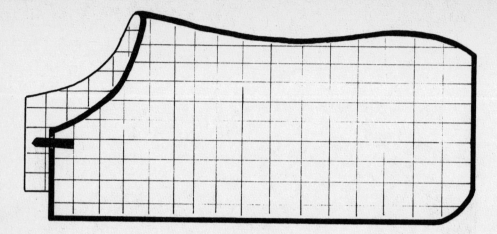

You will need:

Plain or checked cotton or similar weight material according to the materials
chart on page 34.
1 inch (2.5 cm.) wide tape or braid for binding.
Sewing thread to match both the binding and the rug.
Straps and buckles.

To make

1. Cut out one pair of rug shapes. From the material cut out of the neck,
   cut 2 pieces each 5 inches (13 cm.) wide for reinforcement at the front
   neck edge. (Fig. 60)
   (If the remaining pieces from the neck are 10 inches (25 cm.) wide x 15 inches
   (38 cm.) long at the centre, they can be used to make a tail guard).

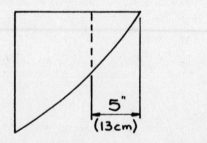

5"
(13cm)

Fig. 60

2. Using thread to match the binding, with the wrong sides of the material
   together, join the centre top seam. Fold the seam to one side and stitch
   down.   (Fig. 61)

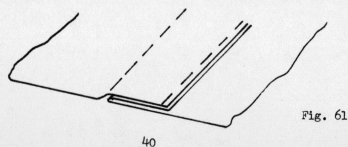

Fig. 61

3. Stitch a strip of binding over the centre top seam, by stitching along each edge of the binding. (Fig. 62)

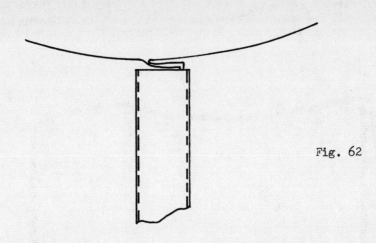

Fig. 62

4. Turn under the curved edges of the reinforcing pieces for the front neck edge, and, using thread to match the rug, stitch this fold in place. With the wrong sides of the material together, stitch the reinforcing pieces to the front neck edge. Put a row of stitching all the way round the curve of the neck to prevent it stretching when it is being bound. (Fig. 63)

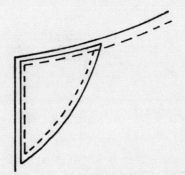

Fig. 63

5. Using thread to match the binding, start at the centre back seam edge and bind the sheet all the way round using Method B as described in Chapter 3.

6. Using thread to match the sheet, stitch fillet string loops on to the inside of the rug at the positions shown on the pattern.

7. Attach a strap and buckle.

8. Make a surcingle as described in Chapter 5.

9. Make a fillet string as described in Chapter 6.

10. Attach a surcingle loop over the centre top binding if required.

EXERCISE SHEET

An exercise sheet is worn for slow work on cold days by a horse which has had its back clipped off. The sheet should cover the area which would be unclipped if the horse had been blanket clipped.

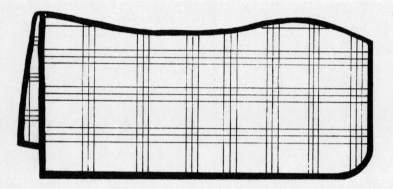

<u>You will need:</u>

Blanket-weight material according to the materials chart on page 34.
<u>Or</u> a travelling rug.

1 inch (2.5 cm.) or 1½ inch (4 cm.) wide tape or braid for binding.
Sewing thread to match both the sheet and the binding.

<u>To make</u>

1. Fold back the front portion of the rug pattern so that it is now to the length required.

   Fold the pattern along its length, approximately half way down, so that it is now at the required depth. (Fig. 64)

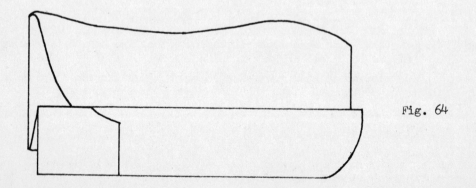

Fig. 64

2. Cut out a pair of exercise sheet shapes from your material.
   (NOTE: Some travelling rugs are loosely woven and soft. If you use one
   of these it may not be necessary to shape the centre top seam as
   the material will mould itself to the horse's back. In this case,
   do not cut along the centre back seam, but stitch binding along it
   anyway to make the sheet look properly finished).

3. Using thread to match the binding, with the wrong sides of the material
   together, join the centre top seam. Fold the seam to one side and stitch
   it down. (Fig. 65)

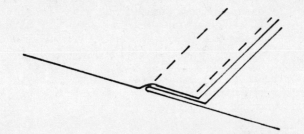

Fig. 65

4. Stitch a strip of binding over the centre top seam. For 1 inch (2.5 cm.)
   wide binding, stitch along each edge of the binding. For 1½ inch (4 cm.)
   wide binding, use 3 rows of stitching. (Fig. 66)

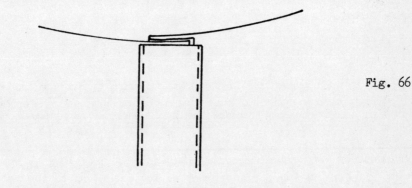

Fig. 66

5. Starting at the centre back edge, bind the sheet, using Method A for
   1½ inch (4 cm.) binding and Method B for 1 inch (2.5 cm.) binding as
   described in Chapter 3.

6. Using thread to match the sheet, stitch fillet string loops on the inside
   of the sheet at the position indicated on the pattern. (Remember that this
   sheet is shorter than your original pattern, and the fillet string loops will
   be closer to the lower edge).

7. Make a fillet string as described in Chapter 6.

Place the exercise sheet on your horse so that when you put your saddle on
top the front edge protrudes beyond the front of the saddle. Fold the front
corners over the saddle panel and trap them under the girth straps.

If the rug moves back when you are riding, you may need to attach girth loops
like those described for the shaped saddle cloth in Chapter 1.

UNBOUND RUG

An unbound rug can be made in single-sided towelling material so that it is slightly warmer than a summer sheet, and more absorbent to sweat. Because of the air pockets formed by the towelling loops, it can be used on a hot horse to help him cool down without getting chilled, in place of an anti-sweat rug and summer sheet together. It should be worn with the towelling side next to the horse.

An unbound blanket-weight rug can be worn under a New Zealand rug to provide extra warmth. This is much safer than the practice often seen of putting a blanket on the horse under his New Zealand rug with the blanket "secured" under the surcingle. If a New Zealand rug is to be worn with an extra lining for more than an hour or so, the lining should be tacked into the rug. If it is to be worn for only a short time, the lining rug can be secured with a surcingle before the New Zealand rug is put on the horse. A very simple surcingle for this purpose can be made by stitching velcro to each end of a strip of material. You may also need to cut slots in the lining rug to pass the leg straps through.

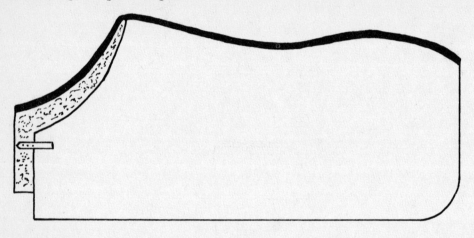

You will need:

Single sided towelling for an absorbent rug according to the materials chart on page 34.
½ inch (1.25 cm.) wide tape to match, sufficiently long to fit along the centre top seam, around the neck edge and make fillet string loops.
Or
Blanket-weight material according to the materials chart on page 34.
Straps and buckles.

To make

1. For an absorbent rug, cut out one pair of rug shapes according to your pattern. For a lining rug, cut out 1 pair of shapes using the rug to be lined as a pattern, but only add a seam allowance to the centre top seam and front edge. Cut the neck, depth and length exactly the same as the rug so that when finished, the lining rug will not be visible under the top rug.

2. From the material cut out of the neck, cut 2 pieces each 5 inches (13 cm.) wide for reinforcement at the front neck edge. (Fig. 67)

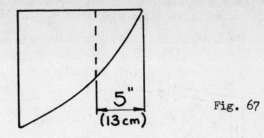

Fig. 67

3. With the wrong sides of the material together, join the centre top seam. (For the towelling rug, the pile side is the wrong side). Fold the seam to one side and stitch it down. (Fig. 68)

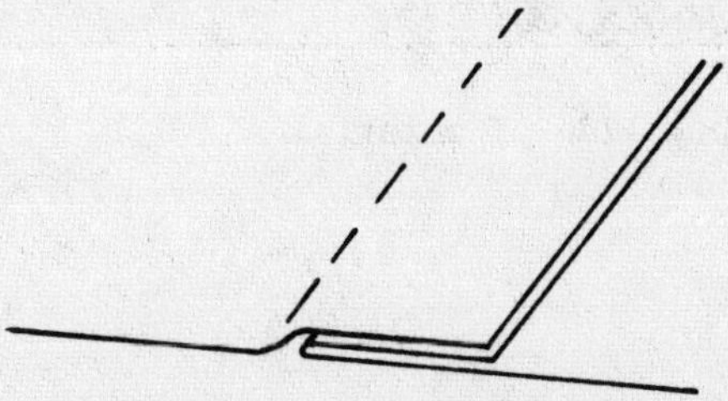

Fig. 68

4. For the absorbent rug only, stitch a strip of $\frac{1}{2}$ inch (1.25 cm.) wide tape over the centre top seam, by stitching along each edge of the binding. (Fig. 69) (Trim the seam before applying the binding).

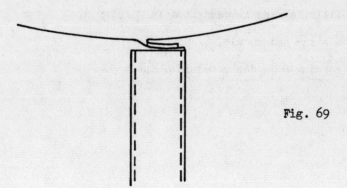

Fig. 69

5. With the wrong sides of the material together, stitch the reinforcing
pieces to the front neck edge.   Put a row of stitching around the curve
of the neck to avoid it stretching when hemming it.   (Fig. 70)

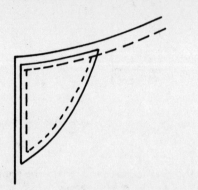

Fig. 70

6. Make a ½ inch (1.25 cm.) single hem to the wrong side all the way round,
and zig-zag machine stitch over the raw edge through to the right side
of the rug. (Fig. 71)

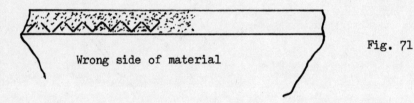

Wrong side of material

Fig. 71

Steps 7 to 9 are for an absorbent rug only.

7. Stitch ½ inch (1.25 cm.) wide tape around the inside of the neck to
cover the zig-zagged raw edge of the towelling, but stitching along
each edge of the binding.

8. Stitch fillet string loops on the inside of the rug at the positions
indicated on the pattern.

9. Make a fillet string as described in Chapter 6.

10. Attach a strap and buckle.

11. Make a surcingle as described in Chapter 5.

LINED NIGHT RUG

A lined night rug can either be made with ready-quilted material, or you can quilt your own. Because of the size of the pieces of material being handled, if you are going to quilt your own, use the minimum amount of stitching required to hold the layers of material together, and put rows of stitching down the length of the material only, about 10 inches (25 cm.) apart.

You will be able to make a thicker rug by quilting your own material than by using ready quilted material.

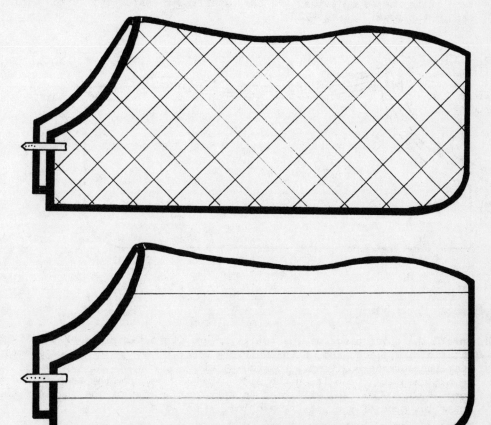

<u>You will need</u>:

Quilted nylon for the top layer and brushed nylon for the lining.

<u>Or</u> Industrial nylon (plain overall nylon) for the top layer, terylene wadding for the padding and calico for the lining.

According to the materials chart on page 34.

2 yards (2 m.) of 35/36 inch (90 cm.) wide nylon dress lining for binding the rug. ¾ yard (0.75 m.) of 35/36 inch (90 cm.) wide nylon dress lining for binding the surcingle.

Straps and buckles.

Sewing thread to match both the rug and the binding.

1. Cut out one pair of rug shapes in the material for the top layer and one
pair of shapes in brushed nylon for the lining, if you are using ready
quilted material, and carry out steps 2 and 3.

Or cut out one pair of rug shapes from the material you have quilted yourself,
and carry out steps 4 to 7.

2. For ready-quilted material, place the right sides of the top layer material
together and the right sides of the lining material together.   Place the
two lining shapes on top of the two outer layer shapes and stitch along the
centre top seam.   (Fig. 72)

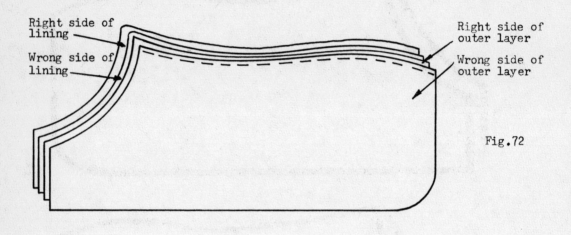

Right side of
lining

Wrong side of
lining

Right side of
outer layer

Wrong side of
outer layer

Fig.72

3. Unfold the outer piece of the top layer and the outer piece of the lining
material and place them, with the wrong sides of the material together, so
that the work is now flat.   Stitch parallel to the centre top seam $\frac{1}{4}$ inch
(0.625 cm.) away from it on the side which will secure the seam inside the
rug.   (Fig. 73)   You will need to roll up one half of the rug to fit it
under the arch of your sewing machine.

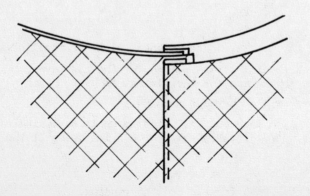

Fig. 73

4. <u>For material which you have quilted yourself</u>, place the right sides of the outer layer material together and fold the lining material out of the way. Place strips of newspaper along the seam line to prevent the sewing machine foot catching in the wadding, and machine along the centre top seam. (Fig. 74) Tear the newspaper away when you have finished stitching.

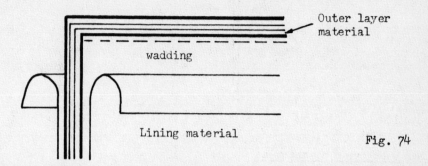

wadding

Outer layer material

Lining material

Fig. 74

5. Fold the seam to one side and tack it down. (Fig. 75)

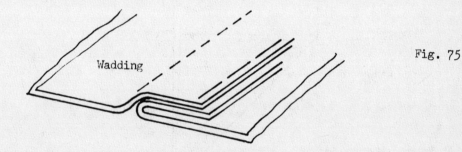

Wadding

Fig. 75

6. Place the lining material over the seam as shown in Fig. 76 and tack this in place.

Fig. 76

Lining material

7. Stitch parallel to the centre seam ¼ inch (0.625 cm.) away from it, on the side which will secure the seam inside the rug. (Fig. 77)

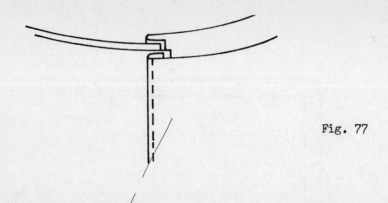

Fig. 77

For both types of material

8. Stitch the lining to the top layer all the way round the edge of the rug, close to the edge.

9. Cut bias strips from the nylon dress lining material, each 4 inches (10 cm.) wide. To find the true bias of the material, fold it as shown in Fig. 78.

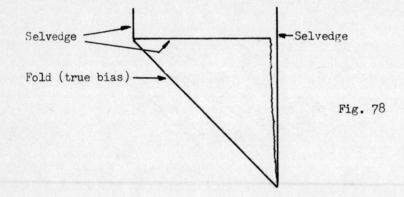

Selvedge

Selvedge

Fold (true bias)

Fig. 78

10. Using thread to match the bias strips, join them together to form a continuous length. (Fig. 79) Press each of the seams open using a warm iron.

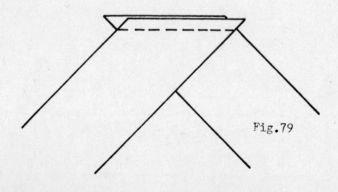

Fig.79

11. Fold and press the bias strip in half down its length so that the seams are on the inside.

12. Starting at the centre back edge of the rug, place the raw edges of the strip on to the right side of the edge of the outer layer material as shown in Fig. 80.   Stitch all the way round ½ inch (1.25 cm.) in from the edge of the rug, but leaving the first ½ inch (1.25 cm.) unstitched.

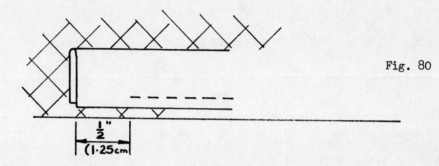

Fig. 80

13. When the starting point has been reached again, fold the first ½ inch (1.25 cm.) over and overlap the bias strip as shown in Fig. 81.

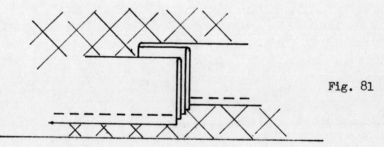

Fig. 81

14. Fold the bias strip round the edge of the rug so that its folded edge is further on to the rug on the lining side than the stitching line already securing it from the other side.   (Fig. 82)   Tack the bias strip in place from the lining side of the rug.

Fig. 82

15. Using thread to match the rug, and with the outer layer of the rug uppermost, stitch around the rug just above the binding strip, so that you stitch through the part of the bias strip which is on the lining side of the rug.   (Fig. 83)

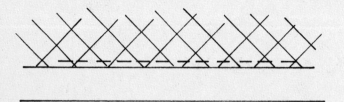

Fig.83

16. Remove the tacking stitches from the binding.

17. Attach a strap and buckle.

18. Make a surcingle from the top layer material (and wadding if you have quilted your own) only as described in Chapter 5.   Bind the surcingle using the same method as used for the rug.

FOAL RUG

Because of the rate at which foals grow, rugs do not fit them for more than a few weeks. If extra seam and hem allowances are made, you can let the rug out so that your foal can wear it for a longer period.

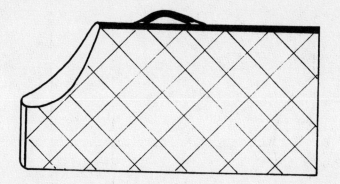

<u>You will need:</u>

Quilted nylon for the top layer.
Brushed nylon for the lining.
1 inch (2.5 cm.) wide tape or braid for binding.

) According to the materials
) chart on page 34.

1½ inch (4 cm.) wide tape or a tail bandage with the tapes removed to use in place of a surcingle.

<u>To make</u>

1. Place the lining material on top of the top layer material with their wrong sides together, and then treat the two pieces of material as if they were one.

2. Fold the material in half, and place the pattern on it as shown. Cut out the rug, but do not cut along the centre top seam. (Fig. 84)

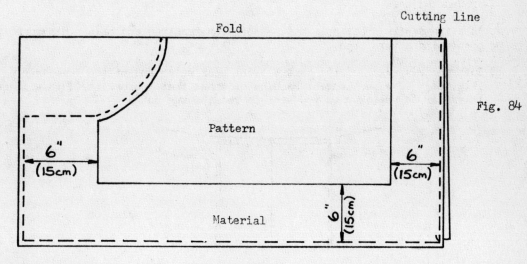

3. Open out the material and tack the pattern shape on to it so that you can use the tack line as a guide for seams and hems. Mark the centre top line (where the material was folded) with tacking stitches. (Fig. 85)

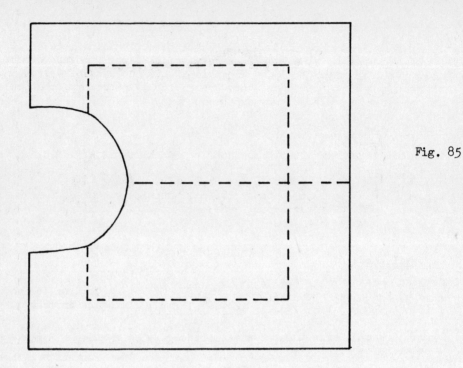

Fig. 85

4. Stitch a strip of 1 inch (1.25 cm.) wide binding along the centre top line of the rug on the outer side material, by stitching along each edge of the binding.

5. Make a surcingle loop from a piece of 1 inch (1.25 cm.) wide tape which is 9 inches (24 cm.) long.

6. Fold in the neck edge. Turn the raw edges under and stitch the hem down around the neck.

7. Join the centre front seam at the position required and press this seam open using a warm iron.

8. Turn the raw edges of the centre front seam under and stitch them down. (Fig. 86) Use the longest machine stitches that you can. (This will make it easier to unpick when you want to let the rug out).

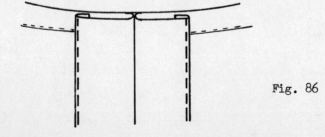

Fig. 86

9. Turn up the hem at the lower and back edges by the amount required.
Turn the raw edges under and stitch them down using long machine
stitches.

To fit the rug on the foal

Slip the neck of the rug over the foal's head.   Tie a piece of $1\frac{1}{2}$ inch
(4 cm.) wide tape, or a tail bandage with the tapes removed, around the
rug instead of a surcingle.   Tie this around the surcingle loop in a bow
so that it cannot slip back along the rug.   If necessary, the bow can be
undone quickly to make removing the rug easy.

To let the rug out

Carefully remove the stitching securing the hems at the lower and back
edges.
Remove all the stitching from the centre front seam.
Rejoin the centre front seam at the new position required.
Turn up the hems by the amount required.

CHAPTER 5

SURCINGLES

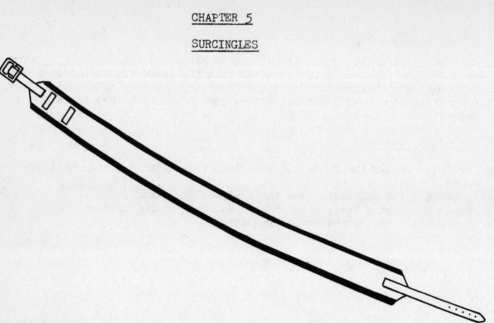

You will need:

Materials to match the rug, according to the materials chart on page 34.
Binding to match the rug, if required.
Sewing thread to match the binding, if required.
Sewing thread to match the rug, if it is unbound.
Straps and buckle.

To make

For a bound rug

1. Cut the material into 3 inch (7.5 cm.) or 4 inch (10 cm.) wide strips,
   depending on the width of the surcingle required. You may have to join
   strips together if one is not long enough. If you have to join strips,
   press the seams open and turn one strip round so that, when two are placed
   together, the seams do not come in the same place.

2. With the wrong sides of the material together, place two strips on top of
   each other.

3. Stitch the two strips together all the way round close to the edge.

4. Bind each side of the strip using the same method as used on the rug.

5. Attach a strap and buckle as described in Chapter 4.

For an unbound rug

1. Cut the material into strips 8 inches (20 cm.) wide. You will need one
   strip, and if one piece of material is not long enough, you will have to
   join two pieces. If so, press the seam open.

2. Fold the strip in half along its length (wrong sides of the material together), and press the fold in place.

3. Fold the raw edges in along the long edge and press. Stitch along both long sides approximately $\frac{1}{4}$ inch (0.625 cm.) in from the edge. (**Fig. 87**)

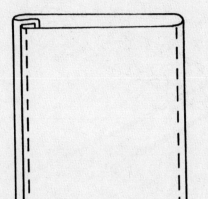

Fig. 87

4. Attach a strap and buckle as described in Chapter 4.

CHAPTER 6

FILLET STRINGS

1. FRENCH KNITTING

You will need:

1 empty wooden cotton reel
4 small nails
1 fine crochet hook or darning needle
knitting yarn

(a) Hammer the nails into one end of the cotton reel an equal distance from the centre hole, to form the corners of a square.

(b) Pass the end of the knitting yarn down the hole so that about 1 inch (2.5 cm.) sticks out from the bottom of the cotton reel. (**Fig.** 88)

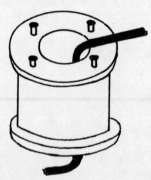

Fig. 88

(c) Wind the yarn around each nail as shown in Fig. 89.

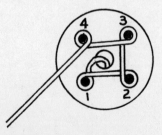

Fig. 89

(d) Pass the yarn around the outside of nail No. 1.   Lift the original loop
    over the yarn and the nail, using the crochet hook or darning needle.
    Pull down on the piece of yarn sticking out from the bottom of the cotton
    reel.

(e) Repeat for each nail in turn, pulling down on the work at every stitch as
    it appears from the bottom of the cotton reel.

(f) When the work measures 1½ yards (1.5 m.) cut the yarn to leave 4 inches
    (10 cm.).   Cast off by passing the cut end of yarn through loops 1, 2 and
    3 only.   Pull a loop of yarn through the loop already on nail 4 and pass
    the free end through this.   Remove the work from the nails and pull the
    casting off piece of yarn tight.

2. PLAITING

(A) Plaited Braid

You will need:

3 x 2½ yards (3 x 2.5 m.) of 1 inch (2.5 cm.) wide braid.
(Total 7½ yards (7.5 m.) of braid).

Single-coloured plait

3-coloured plait

Using a warm iron, press the braid in half down its length.   Cut the braid
into 3 equal lengths of each 2½ yards (2.5 m.).

Place one end of each of the 3 pieces together. Knot them.
Hook the knot over a suitable fixed object (such as a nail or hook), and
keeping the braid flat, plait to within 4 inches (10 cm.) of the end.
Knot the ends together.

(B) Plaited Tape

You will need:

3 x 2½ yards (3 x 2.5 m.) of 1 inch (2.5 cm.) wide tape.
(Total 7½ yards (7.5 m.) of tape).

Single-coloured plait

3-coloured plait

Cut the tape into 3 equal lengths each of 2½ yards (2.5 m.).
Place one end of each piece together and knot.
Hook the knot over a suitable fixed object (such as a nail or hook).
Allowing the tape to form folds naturally down its length, plait to within
4 inches (10 cm.) of the end.   Knot the ends together.

(C) <u>Plaited Knitting Yarn</u>

Single-coloured plait

3-coloured plait

Make 3 bundles of double knitting yarn each 6 strands thick and 2½ yards
(2.5 m.) long.

Place one end of each bundle together.   Knot them.
Hook the knotted end over a suitable fixed object (such as a nail or hook),
and plait to within 4 inches (10 cm.) of the end.   Knot the ends together.

(D) <u>Plaited Cord</u>

<u>You will need:</u>

3 x 5 yards (3 x 4.5 m.) of thin cord.
(Total 15 yards (13.5 m.) of cord).

Cut the cord into 6 equal lengths of 2½ yards (2.25 m.).
Place one end of each of the 6 pieces together and knot them.
Hook the knot over a suitable fixed object (such as a nail or hook).
Divide the cord into 3 groups of 2 cords.
Keeping the cords flat, side by side, plait to within 4 inches (10 cm.)
of the end.   Knot the ends together.

3. READY-MADE CORD

   You will need:

   1½ yards (1.5 m.) of pyjama or similar thick cord of minimum diameter
   ¼ inch (6 mm.).

   Tie a knot in each end.

4. HOME-MADE CORD

This will require help from another person.

   Find a ½ lb. (0.25 kg.) weight (e.g. a stone or weight from a set of scales).

   If there is no ring or hook on the object you are using for a weight, wind
   string around it securely so that a hook can be attached.

   Make a hook from a suitable piece of metal, e.g. a stout piece of wire,
   a skewer or a steel knitting needle, and attach this to the weight. (Fig. 90)

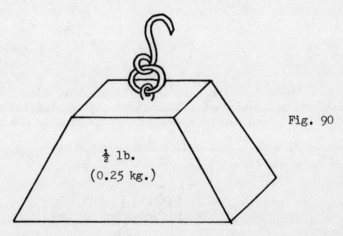

½ lb.
(0.25 kg.)

Fig. 90

The amount of yarn you will need is mentioned under each type of cord.

Tie one end of the bundle of yarn to be corded to a suitable fixed object,
such as a door knob or a hook.   (You will need to stand a considerable
distance away from this, and if there is insufficient space indoors, the
cord will have to be made outdoors).

Attach the other end of the bundle of yarn to a pencil or stick.   (Fig. 91)

Fig. 91

By turning the pencil round and round, twist the yarn until kinks appear
in the twists.

Ask your assistant to hang the weight half way down the length of the work
so that the kinks straighten out, and to hold the weight at this point.
(Fig. 92)

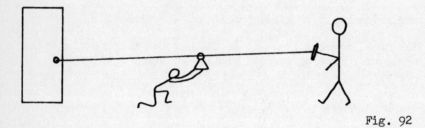

Fig. 92

Carefully move the end of the cord which is attached to the pencil to
meet the end which is attached to the fixed object, asking your assistant
to ensure that no kinks occur in the cord by pulling on the weight.

Detach the end from the fixed object and hold the two ends together so
that the weight can hang freely.   (Fig. 93)

Fig. 93

Ask your assistant to let go of the weight and allow the cord to twist naturally.

Remove the pencil or stick, and knot each end of the cord.

(A) Random-grouped cord

 Random-dyed yarn

 2-colour random-grouped yarn

 Single-coloured yarn

Make a bundle of 10 strands of double knitting yarn 4½ yards (4.25 m.) long, and twist into a cord.

(B) Two-coloured knitting yarn (colours together)

Make a bundle of 5 strands each of two colours of double knitting yarn (10 strands in all), 4½ yards (4.25 m.) long.   Place the two bundles side by side and twist into a cord.

(C) Twisted cord

Take 9 yards (8.5 m.) of thin cord.   Fold the cord in half and twist into a cord.

(D) <u>Two-coloured knitting yarn</u> (colours separated)

Make 2 bundles of 10 strands each of two colours of double knitting yarn 2¼ yards (2.25 m.) long (20 strands in all). Knot the bundles into one continuous length of 4½ yards (4.5 m.) and twist into a cord.

(E) <u>Double twisted yarn</u>

Make a bundle of 5 strands each of two colours of double knitting yarn 6¾ yards (6.5 m.) long. (10 strands in all).

Twist each colour separately into a cord, making sure that the direction of twist is the same on both.

Knot the two cords together to form a continuous length 4½ yards (4.25 m.) long, and twist again to form a thicker cord, making sure that the direction of twist is the same as for the original ones.

CHAPTER 7

TAIL GUARD

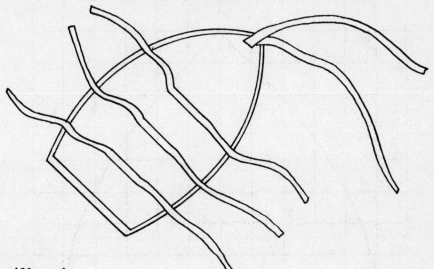

You will need:

7 yards (6.5 m.) of 1 inch (2.5 cm.) wide tape or braid for binding.

<u>Either</u> 1 piece of foam 15 inches (38 cm.) x 10 inches (25 cm.) x ¼ inch
(0.625 cm.) thick.

2 pieces of cotton or similar fabric each 15 inches (38 cm.) x 10 inches
(25 cm.).

<u>Or</u> 2 pieces of woollen blanket or similar weight material each 15 inches
(38 cm.) x 10 inches (25 cm.).

Sewing thread to match the binding.

(NOTE: The pieces of material left over after cutting out the neck of a rug
may be of sufficient size).

To make

1. <u>Either</u> (a) Cut out 1 piece of foam and 2 pieces of cotton material to
the pattern shown. Place the foam between the two pieces of
cotton and sew the three layers together by stitching close to
the edge.

<u>Or</u> (b) Cut out 2 pieces of blanket-weight material to the pattern shown,
and place one on top of the other. Sew them together by
stitching round the edge.

2. Cut a sufficient length of binding to go round the edge of the material.
Fold it in half lengthways and press the fold in place with a warm iron.

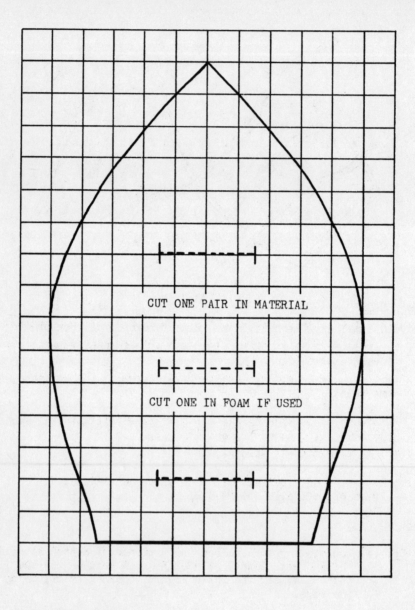

CUT ONE PAIR IN MATERIAL

CUT ONE IN FOAM IF USED

EACH SQUARE REPRESENTS 1 INCH (2.5 CM.)

CUT AROUND SOLID LINE ONLY.

3. Starting at the top point of the tail guard, sew the tape around the edge of the work so that the fold is lying on the edge of the material.   (Fig. 94)

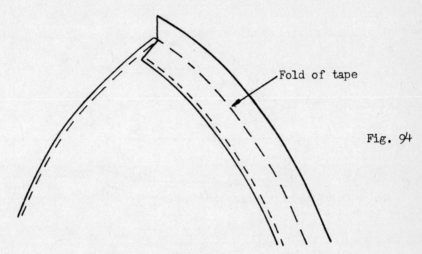

Fold of tape

Fig. 94

4. Turn the tail guard over and fold the tape around the edge of the work. Stitch the tape down so that the tail guard is now bound all the way round.   (Fig. 95)

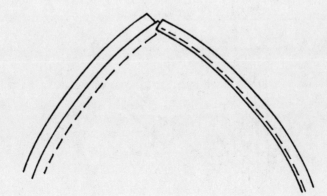

Fig. 95

5. Cut 3 pieces of tape each 36 inches (90 cm.) long and stitch them at the positions shown on the pattern so that the free ends are approximately the same length. (Fig. 96)

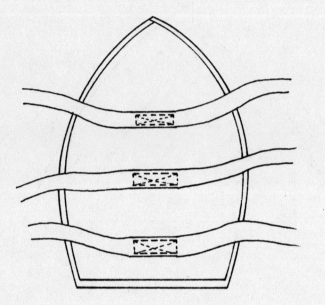

Fig. 96

6. Fold the remaining piece of tape in half across the centre and press the fold in place.

   Fold each half back again 1 inch (2.5 cm.) from the centre fold and press again. (Fig. 97)

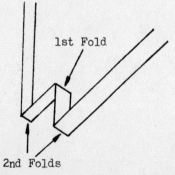

1st Fold

2nd Folds

Fig. 97

7. Place the centre fold over the point of the tail guard, and stitch in place.   (Fig. 98)

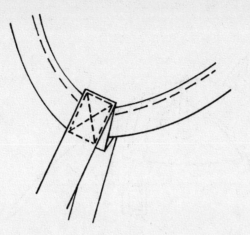

Fig. 98

TO FIT THE TAIL GUARD ON YOUR HORSE FOR TRAVELLING

A tail bandage can easily slip when your horse is travelling, and this can result in raw patches being rubbed in his tail.   A tail guard should not slip if you secure it properly.

If your horse does not wear a rug when travelling, you can still fit a tail guard by simply putting a surcingle or roller on him and securing the tail guard to this.

Apply a tail bandage to your horse's tail.   Tie the long tapes of the tail guard around the surcingle of the rug, so that the top of the tail guard will cover the root of his tail.   Wrap the tail guard around the top of his tail and tie it in place by winding each of the three tapes in turn around under his tail and tying a bow on top.   (Fig. 99)

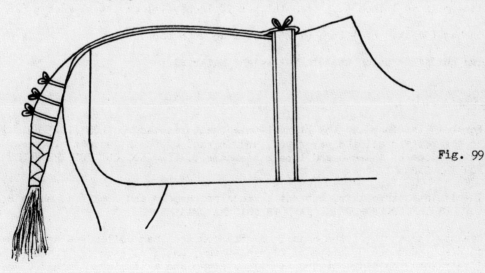

Fig. 99

CHAPTER 8

POLL GUARD

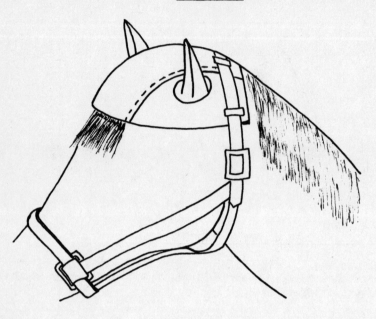

You will need:

1 piece of simulated sheepskin 19 inches (48 cm.) x 10 inches (25 cm.)

1 piece of blanket-weight material 20 inches (51 cm.) x 11 inches (28 cm.)

1 piece of foam 1 inch (2.5 cm.) thick x 20 inches (51 cm.) x 11 inches (28 cm.)

22 inches (56 cm.) of $\frac{1}{2}$ inch (1.25 cm.) wide seam tape.

Sewing thread to match the blanket-weight material.

To make

1. For both the foam and the blanket-weight material add $\frac{1}{2}$ inch (1.25 cm.) to the pattern all the way round, and in each of these two materials cut out 1 piece of shape A and 1 pair of shape B.   DO NOT CUT OUT THE HOLES FOR THE EARS.

2. In simulated sheepskin, cut out 1 piece of shape A and 1 pair of shape B. CUT OUT THE HOLES FOR THE EARS IN THIS MATERIAL ONLY.

3. Measure the width of the headpiece strap on the head collar you are going to use.   Cut out 3 strips of blanket-weight material each 1$\frac{1}{2}$ inches (4 cm.) longer than the width of the headpiece strap and measuring 2 inches (5 cm.) wide.

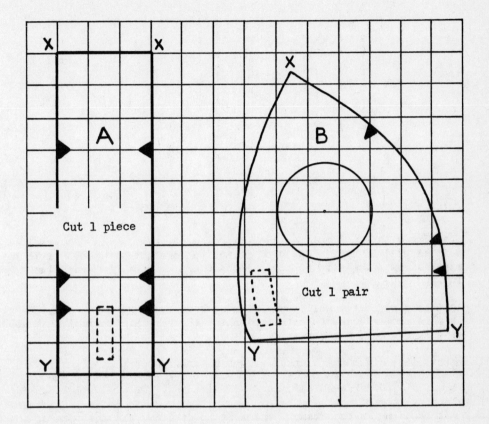

EACH SQUARE REPRESENTS 1 INCH (2.5 CM.)

CUT AROUND SOLID LINE ONLY

Add ½ inch (1.25 cm.) all the way round each pattern piece when
cutting out the foam and the blanket-weight material.

The finished measurements for this poll guard are:-

      16 inches (41 cm.) over the head collar head piece.

      20 inches (51 cm.) round the forehead.

      4½ inches (11.5 cm.) between the ears.

Any adjustment to these measurements should be made to pattern
piece A.

Trim seam to within
$\frac{1}{4}$ inch (0.625 cm.) of
stitching line.

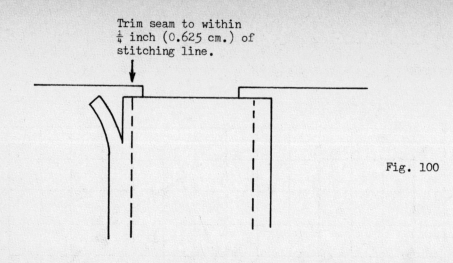

Fig. 100

4. Starting with the simulated sheepskin shapes, overlap the material along
   seam XY by 1 inch (2.5 cm.) and stitch to form a flat seam.   Trim the
   material on piece A to within $\frac{1}{4}$ inch (0.625 cm.) of the seam line as shown
   in Fig. 100.

5. As this part of the poll guard fits close to your horse's head, check that
   it fits properly and that the holes for the ears are correct.   Make any
   adjustments before going on.

6. Repeat step 4 for the blanket-weight material.

7. Repeat step 4 for the foam, but place $\frac{1}{2}$ inch (1.25 cm.) wide seam tape
   along the top of the seam before sewing to prevent the sewing machine
   foot catching in the foam.   There is no need to trim the seam of the foam.

8. Fold the 3 strips of blanket-weight material as shown in Fig. 101, and
   stitch down the centre of the length of each.

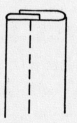

Fig. 101

9. Place these strips on the blanket-weight material at the positions shown
   on the pattern, and stitch down $\frac{1}{2}$ inch (1.25 cm.) at each end (Fig. 102).
   These strips form slots for the headcollar, and the unstitched centre
   portion should be $\frac{1}{2}$ inch (1.25 cm.) longer than the width of your headcollar
   strap.

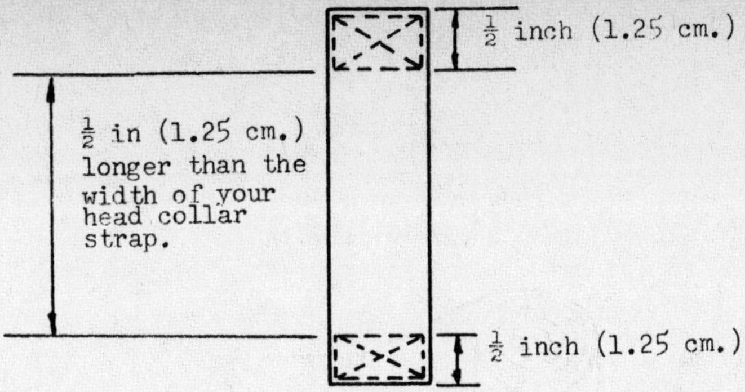

½ inch (1.25 cm.)

½ in (1.25 cm.) longer than the width of your head collar strap.

Fig. 102

½ inch (1.25 cm.)

10. Place the foam shape between the simulated sheepskin and the blanket-weight material, so that the simulated sheepskin forms the underside of the poll guard, and the right side of both the simulated sheepskin and the blanket-weight material are outermost.

11. With the simulated sheepskin uppermost, stitch through the three layers round close to the edge. Trim off any untidy material around the edge to give a neat finish.

12. With the simulated sheepskin side uppermost, stitch around the holes for the ears through all three layers close to the edge of the holes. Cut out the ear holes in the foam and blanket-weight material. Trim away any untidy material to give a neat finish around the ears.

(Note: There is no need to bind the poll guard, but this may be done, if desired, using the method described for the tail guard in Chapter 7).

BANDAGES

(With Velcro or tape fastenings)

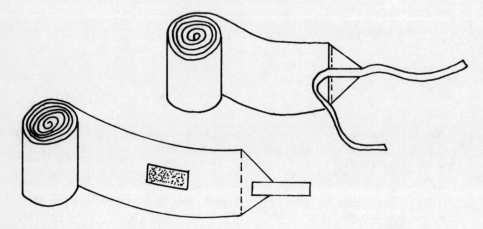

Many commercially produced bandages are only 6 feet (180 cm.) long.
You will find them easier to put on if they are at least 7 feet 6 inches
(235 cm.) long.

The widths in which fabrics are available mean that you can cut more than
one set of 4 bandages from a length, which can be very helpful if they are
in frequent use.

If only one set of bandages is required, the fabric left over can be used
to make other items.

The chart below shows various combinations of bandage widths which can be
cut from each width of fabric, assuming that the whole piece of material
is to be used for bandages.

WIDTH OF MATERIAL	NUMBER OF SETS OF 4 BANDAGES	WIDTH OF BANDAGES
36 inches (92 cm.)	2	$4\frac{1}{2}$ inches (11.5 cm.)
	1	4 inches (10 cm.)
	1	5 inches (13 cm.)
45 inches (115 cm.)	3	$3\frac{3}{4}$ inches (9.5 cm.)
	$2\frac{1}{2}$	$4\frac{1}{2}$ inches (11.5 cm.)
54 inches (136 cm.)	3	$4\frac{1}{2}$ inches (11.5 cm.)
	1	4 inches (10 cm.)
	1	$4\frac{1}{2}$ inches (11.5 cm.)
	1	5 inches (13 cm.)

Continued.........

Blanket – 70 inches (180 cm.) x 90 inches (230 cm.)	2	4 inches (10 cm.)
	1	4½ inches (11.5 cm.)
	1	5 inches (13 cm.)
	1	4 inches (10 cm.)
	3	4½ inches (11.5 cm.)
Blanket – 90 inches (230 cm.) x 100 inches (250 cm.)	5	4½ inches (11.5 cm.)
	1	4 inches (10 cm.)
	3	4½ inches (11.5 cm.)
	1	5 inches (13 cm.)
	2	4 inches (10 cm.)
	1	4½ inches (11.5 cm.)
	2	5 inches (13 cm.)

<u>You will need</u>:

2¾ yards (2.5 m.) of woollen or synthetic blanket-weight material.

<u>Or</u> 1 blanket 90 inches (230 cm.) x 70 inches (180 cm.)

<u>Or</u> 1 blanket 100 inches (250 cm.) x 90 inches (230 cm.)

<u>AND for each set of bandages</u>

<u>Either</u>: 4 yards (4 m.) of ½ inch (1.25 cm.) wide tape.
<u>Or</u>:   20 inches (50 cm.) of heavy duty Velcro.

<u>To make</u>

1. Cut the material into strips of the width(s) chosen.
2. Fold one end of each strip as shown in Fig. 103 and stitch into place.

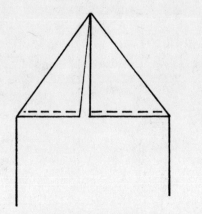

Fig. 103

3. Cut the tape into 1 yard (1 m.) lengths.

4. Find the middle of each length of tape and stitch this in place over the folded down edges as shown in Fig. 104.   The two free ends of tape should be approximately the same length.

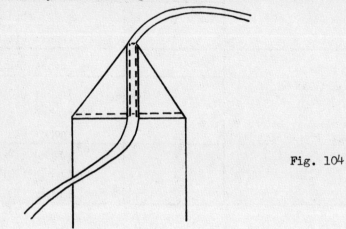

Fig. 104

For bandages with Velcro fastenings

5. Cut the Velcro into 5 inch (12.5 cm.) lengths and separate each of the two halves.

6. With the folded down edges of the material on the underside of the work, place one piece of Velcro, with its sticking face down, on to the end of the bandage, leaving approximately 4 inches (10 cm.) protruding beyond the point.   Stitch the Velcro in place as shown in Fig. 105.

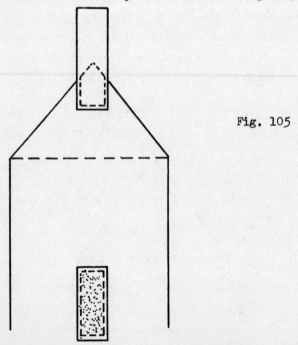

Fig. 105

76

7. Stitch the partnering piece of Velcro on to the same side of the bandage
   as the first, with its sticking face up, leaving approximately 5 inches
   (13 cm.) between this piece and its partner.   (Fig. 105).

(NOTE: The distance between the pieces of Velcro may need to be adjusted,
       depending on the size of your horse's legs and the type of padding
       you use under the bandage.
       5 inches (11.5 cm.) between the pieces if Velcro should be sufficient
       for a horse with 8 to 9 inches of bone).

CHAPTER 10

YORKSHIRE BOOTS

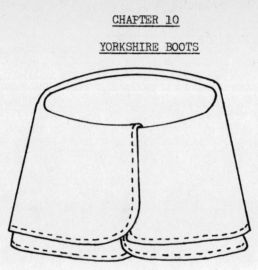

You will need:

For **EACH** boot: 2 pieces of blanket-weight material each 12 inches (30 cm.) x 9 inches (22.5 cm.)

1 yard (1 m.) of 1 inch (2.5 cm.) wide tape.

To make

1. Cut out 2 pieces of material to the shape shown on the pattern.

2. With the wrong sides of the material together, place the shapes on top of each other, and stitch them together, close to the edge.

3. Find the middle of the length of tape and stitch this at the position shown on the pattern. (Fig. 106). The two free ends of tape should be approximately the same length.

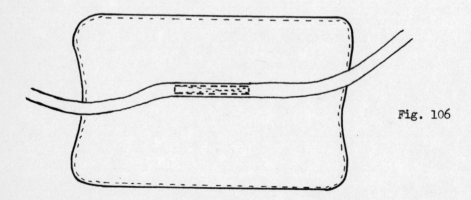

Fig. 106

Now make another boot to match the first.

PATTERN 7   -   YORKSHIRE BOOTS

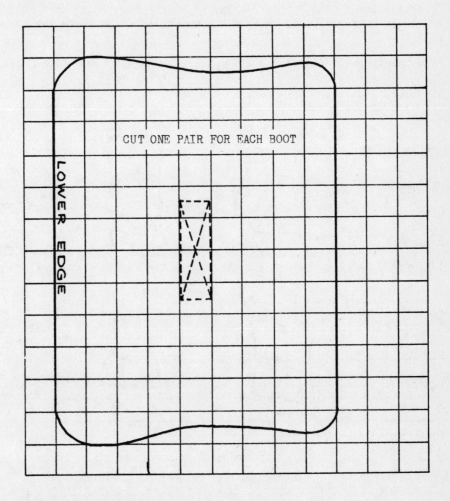

CUT ONE PAIR FOR EACH BOOT

LOWER EDGE

EACH SQUARE REPRESENTS 1 INCH (2.5 CM.)

CUT AROUND SOLID LINE ONLY.

<u>TO FIT THE BOOT ON YOUR HORSE</u>

Place the boot around your horse's leg so that the tape can be tied around just above his fetlock joint, with the edges of the boot overlapping on the outside of his leg.

Bring the tapes around from the inside of the leg, cross them over at the outside of the leg, and tie in a bow on the inside.   Tuck the loops and ends in.

Fold the top half down to form a double layer over the fetlock joint.

<u>Inside of leg</u>

<u>Outside of leg</u>

Fig. 107

CHAPTER 11

BRUSHING BOOTS

NOTE: The boots are made as a pair, so that, when finished, one is a mirror
image of the other.

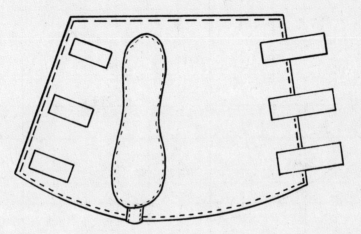

You will need:

Front pair: 2 pieces of blanket-weight material each 11 inches (28 cm.)
             x 9 inches (23 cm.).
             2 pieces of leatherette (upholstery vinyl) or soft leather
             each 8 inches (21 cm.) x 3 inches (8 cm.).

Rear pair: 2 pieces of blanket-weight material each 13 inches (33 cm.)
             x 10 inches (25 cm.).
             2 pieces of leatherette or soft leather each 8 inches (21 cm.)
             x 3 inches (8 cm.)

For each
boot: 12 inches (30 cm.) of heavy duty Velcro.
             3 inches (7.5 cm.) of ½ inch (1.25 cm.) wide tape.
             Foam pieces or old nylon tights for padding.

To make

1. For a pair of boots, cut out one pair of shape A in blanket-weight material
   and one pair of shape B in leatherette or soft leather.

The following instructions are for one boot

2. Stitch a flat dart in the blanket-weight material at the position shown
   on the pattern.   (Fig. 108)

PATTERN 8   -   BRUSHING BOOTS

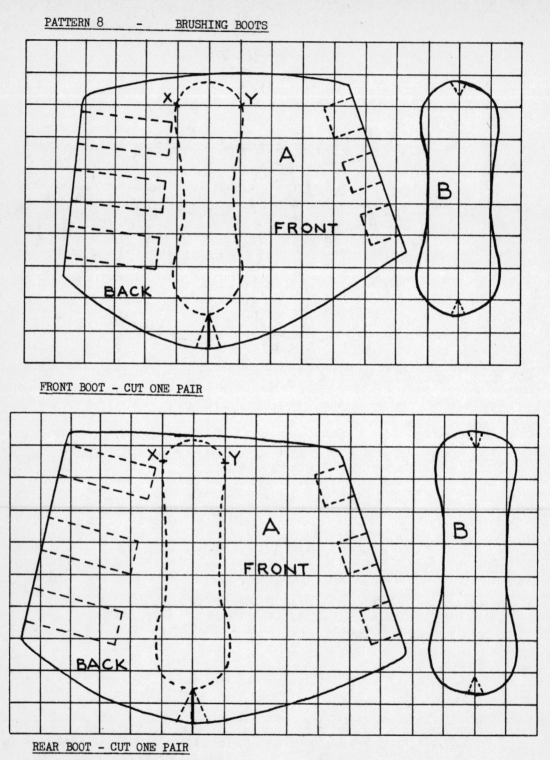

FRONT BOOT - CUT ONE PAIR

REAR BOOT - CUT ONE PAIR

EACH SQUARE REPRESENTS 1 INCH (2.5 CM.)   CUT AROUND SOLID LINE ONLY.

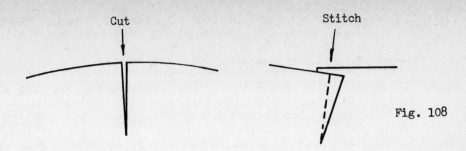

Cut   Stitch

Fig. 108

3. Trim the dart close to the stitching line, and then stitch round shape A close to the edge to prevent fraying.

4. Cover the dart with tape on both sides of the work, by folding the tape over the edge of the material and stitching through all layers as shown in Fig. 109.

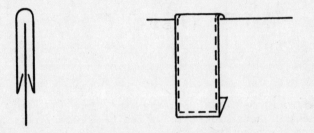

Fig. 109

5. Stitch darts in the leatherette or soft leather at the positions shown on the pattern. (Fig. 110)

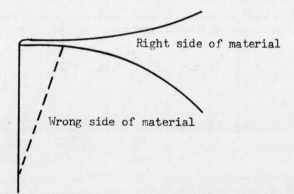

Right side of material

Wrong side of material

Fig. 110

6. Place the leatherette on the blanket-weight shape and stitch down from point X, around the bottom and up to point Y, leaving the top open for stuffing. (You will probably need to place strips of tissue paper or newspaper over the leatherette to enable the foot of your sewing machine to slide. Tear this away when the stitching is finished).

7. Stuff the space between the leatherette and the main piece of material firmly with foam pieces, or old nylon tights which have been cut into small pieces. (Discard the toes and waistband). Finish stitching the leatherette in position from point Y, around the top to point X.

8. Cut the Velcro into 4 inch (10 cm.) long pieces. Separate each of the two halves, and stitch 3 pieces of Velcro, with their sticking faces down, to the front edge of the boot at the positions shown on the pattern. (Fig. 111)

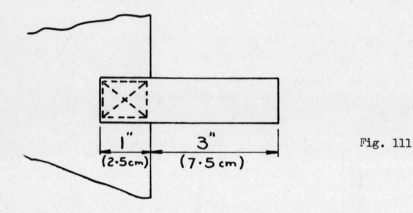

Fig. 111

9. Cut the partnering pieces of Velcro down to 3 inch (7.5 cm.) lengths, and, with their sticking faces up, stitch these to the back edge of the boot at the positions shown on the pattern. (Fig. 112)

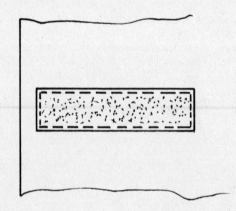

Fig. 112

Make a second boot as a mirror image of the first, reversing the pattern pieces and fastenings.

CHAPTER 12

TRAVELLING BOOTS

(With or without coronet protection)

NOTE: The boots are made as a pair, so that, when finished, one is a mirror image of the other.

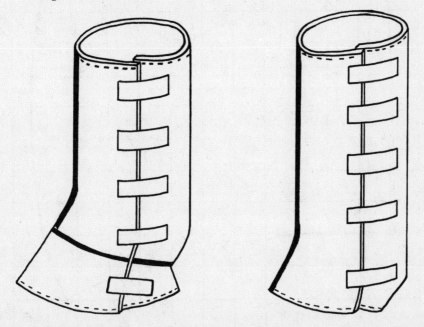

These boots could also be made with leatherette (upholstery vinyl) for the outer layer, in which case replace half of the pieces of blanket-weight materials with leatherette.

For boots without heel and coronet protection, use Pattern Shapes A and B

For one pair of boots, you will need:

4 pieces of blanket-weight material each 20 inches (51 cm.) x 16 inches (40 cm.)

2 pieces of ½ inch (1.25 cm.) thick foam each 20 inches (51 cm.) x 16 inches (40 cm.)

For front boots: 36 inches (90 cm.) of heavy duty Velcro.

For rear boots: 44 inches (110 cm.) of heavy duty Velcro.

1½ yards (1.5 m.) of ½ inch (1.25 cm.) wide tape or braid.

Sewing thread to match the tape, the main material, and binding if used.

Optional binding: 3½ yards (3.5 m.) of 1 inch (2.5 cm.) wide tape or braid.

For boots with heel and coronet protection, use Pattern Shapes A, B and C.

For one pair of boots, you will need:

4 pieces of blanket-weight material each 20 inches (51 cm.) x 16 inches (40 cm.)

4 pieces of blanket-weight material each 12 inches (31 cm.) x 13 inches (33 cm.)

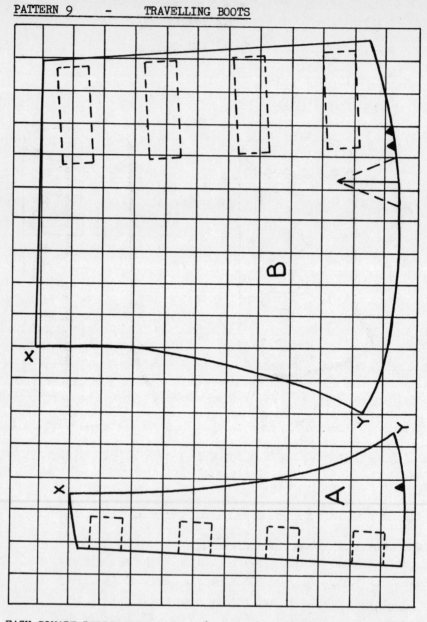

EACH SQUARE REPRESENTS 1 INCH (2.5 CM.)   CUT AROUND SOLID LINE ONLY.

The pattern is for a leg measuring:-
       9 inches (23 cm.) round under the knee or hock.
       11 inches (28 cm.) around the widest part of the fetlock joint.
       11 inches (28 cm.) long, from just below the knee or hock to the
                          narrowest part of the pastern.
Alter the length by adding or subtracting at the top edge.
Alter the distance round the boot by dividing the difference by 4 and
adding or subtracting this amount from both sides of piece A and both
sides of piece B.   The list of materials is sufficient for a boot
measuring up to 16 inches (40 cm.) long and 14 inches (35 cm.) wide.

TRAVELLING BOOTS (Coronet protection)

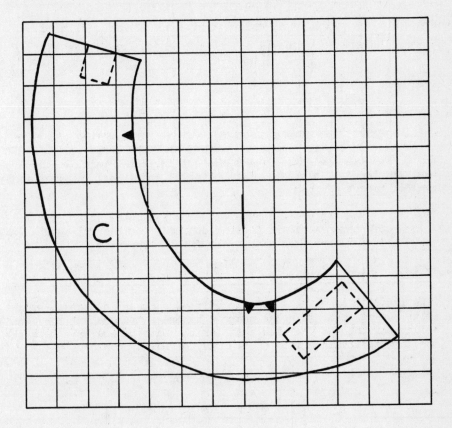

EACH SQUARE REPRESENTS 1 INCH (2.5 CM.)

CUT AROUND SOLID LINE ONLY.

The pattern is for a leg measuring 11 inches (28 cm.) around the
widest part of the fetlock joint.

Alter the distance round the boot by dividing the difference by 2 and
adding or subtracting this amount at each end of piece C.

2 pieces of ½ inch (1.25 cm.) thick foam each 20 inches (51 cm.) x 16 inches (40 cm.)
2 pieces of ½ inch (1.25 cm.) thick foam each 12 inches (31 cm.) x 13 inches (33 cm.)

For front boots: 44 inches (110 cm.) of heavy duty Velcro.
For rear boots: 52 inches (130 cm.) of heavy duty Velcro.
3 yards (3 m.) of ½ inch (2.5 cm.) wide tape.
Sewing thread to match tape, main material and binding, if used.
Optional binding: 4½ yards (4 m.) of 1 inch (2.5 cm.) wide tape or braid.

To make

For one pair of boots:

1. Cut two pairs each of shapes A and B from the larger pieces of blanket-weight
   material, and 1 pair of shapes A and B from the larger pieces of foam.
   For boots with heel and coronet protection, cut 2 pairs of shape C from the
   smaller pieces of blanket-weight material and 1 pair of shape C from the
   smaller pieces of foam.

   (NOTE: If you are using leatherette for the outer layer, cut out 1 pair
            of shapes A, B and C (if required) from blanket-weight material,
            1 pair from foam and 1 pair from leatherette).

The following instructions are for one boot made from blanket-weight material only.

2. Take one pair of shape A and one pair of shape B in blanket-weight material.
   Using a flat seam, join one shape A to one shape B along the seam XY.   Make
   a flat dart at the position shown on the pattern and trim both the seam and
   the dart to within ¼ inch (0.625 cm.) of the stitching line.   (Fig. 113)

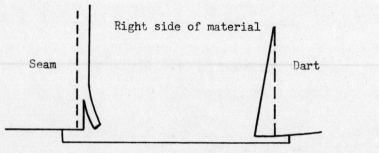

Fig. 113

3. Repeat for the partnering shape A and shape B in blanket-weight material.

4. Repeat for one shape A and one shape B in foam, but tack the dart and seam
   only.   Do not trim the dart or the seam.

5. With the wrong sides of the material together, place the foam between the
   pieces of blanket-weight material, making sure that the seams and darts are
   matched together.

6. Stitch through all three layers down the seam line.

7. Stitch the three layers together all the way round close to the edge.

8. Cut a piece of tape 5 inches (13 cm.) long. Cover the dart with the tape on both sides of the work, by folding the tape over the edge. Stitch through all layers. (Fig. 114)

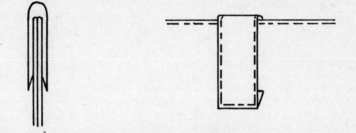

Fig. 114

9. Cover the seams XY on both sides of the work with tape, by first stitching a piece of tape along the seam on the inside of the work, and then stitching a piece of tape down the seam on the outside of the work.

For boots without heel and coronet protection, omit steps 10 to 12.

10. For boots with heel and coronet protection, with the wrong sides of the material together, place 1 piece of foam shape C between one pair of blanket-weight material shape C. Stitch all the way round through the three layers, close to the edge.

11. Using a flat seam, join shape C to the lower edge of the boot so that the notches marked on the pattern match. Trim the seam on the outer surface of the boot to within $\frac{1}{4}$ inch (0.625 cm.) of the stitching line.

12. Cover the seam, on both sides of the work, with tape as described in Step 7.

13. If you wish, bind the boot with the 1 inch (2.5 cm.) wide binding, using Method A as described in Chapter 3.

14. Cut the Velcro into 4 inch (10 cm.) strips, and separate the two halves of each strip.

15. For a front boot use 4 strips for the leg and 1 strip for the coronet protection.

For a rear boot use 5 strips for the leg and 1 strip for the coronet protection.

Stitch the Velcro on to the outer surface of the boot, with the strips equally spaced down the length of the boot. Stitch as shown in Fig. 115.

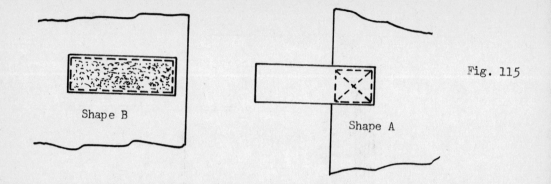

Fig. 115

Shape B

Shape A

Make a second boot as a mirror image of the first, reversing the pattern pieces and fastenings.

CHAPTER 13

KNEE BOOTS

Note: The boots are made as a pair, so that, when finished, one is a mirror
image of the other.

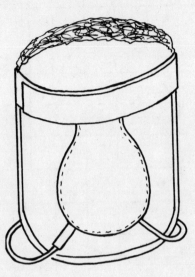

You will need:

Plasticene.

Newspaper.

Wallpaper paste.

Fabric adhesive.

2 pieces of blanket-weight material each 10½ inches (27 cm.) x 8 inches (21 cm.).

2 pieces of matching or contrasting blanket-weight material each 6 inches
(15 cm.) x 9 inches (23 cm.)

2½ yards (2.25 m.) of 1½ inch (4 cm.) wide tape or braid for binding.

20 inches (50 cm.) of 1 inch (2.5 cm.) Velcro.

14 inches (36 cm.) of 1 inch (2.5 cm.) wide strong elastic.

2 pieces of simulated sheepskin each 15 inches (38 cm.) x 4 inches (10 cm.).

2 pieces of ½ inch (1.25 cm.) thick foam each 8 inches (20 cm.) x 1 inch (2.5 cm.).

Sewing thread to match the smaller pieces of blanket-weight material and the binding.

To make

1. Using plasticene, make a dome-shaped mould to match the shape shown on the
pattern.   The height of the dome should be approximately ¾ inch (2 cm.),
and should start about ¼ inch (0.625 cm.) in from the edge.   (Fig. 116)

91

PATTERN 10   -   KNEE BOOTS

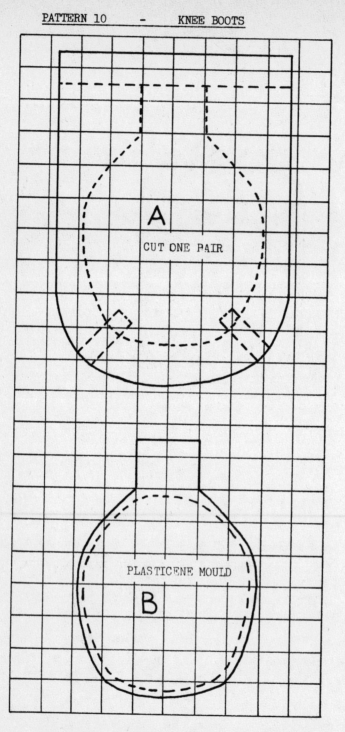

EACH SQUARE REPRESENTS 1 INCH (2.5 CM.)
CUT AROUND SOLID LINE ONLY.

Fig. 116

2. Mix sufficient thick wallpaer paste to fill a 1 lb. (450 grm.) jam jar.

3. Tear the newspaper into pieces large enough to cover the plasticene mould completely and overlap the edges.

4. Smear the top of the plasticene mould thickly with wallpaper paste, and press 1 piece of newspaper down on to the mould. Smooth it down so that it takes up the shape of the plasticene, and soaks up the wallpaper paste. Smear wallpaper paste over the top of this and add another piece of newspaper.
Repeat until 10 layers of newspaper have been pressed and smoothed on to the mould.
There must be no air bubbles in the newspaper and it must be very smooth. Leave the newspaper on the plasticene for 3 or 4 days in a warm place, until the newspaper is completely dry.

5. Trim the edges of the newspaper caste close to the outer edge of the plasticene mould and remove the caste from the plasticene.

   Make a second caste to match.

6. From the larger pieces of blanket-weight material cut out one pair of shape A. Cut the binding in half - one piece for each boot.

The following instructions are for one boot:

7. Bind the two sides and lower edge, using method A as described in Chapter 3.

8. Stitch the rest of this piece of binding in half down its length.

9. Cut a 2 inch (5 cm.) piece of Velcro. Separate the two halves. Stitch one piece to one end of the folded piece of tape, with its sticking face up.

10. Stitch the other piece of Velcro on to the lower, outer edge of the bound material at the position shown on the pattern, with its sticking face up, on the right side of the work. (Fig. 117)

11. Cut the folded tape to about 16 inches (41 cm.) long overall, and stitch the end without the piece of Velcro attached to the lower inner edge of the bound material in the position shown on the pattern, on the right side of the work. (Fig. 117) (If you now lay the tape flat, the Velcro should be on the underside).

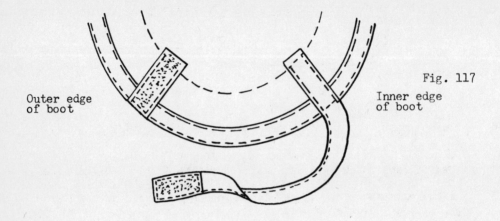

Fig. 117

Outer edge
of boot

Inner edge
of boot

12. Using fabric adhesive, stick one of the smaller pieces of blanket-weight
    material over the top of one of the newspaper castes.   Trim the material
    so that about ¼ inch (0.5 cm.) protrudes all the way round the caste.

13. Using fabric adhesive, stick the underside of the paper caste on to the
    right side of the bound material at the position shown on the pattern.
    Ensure that where the material is stuck to the caste it is smooth and
    free from creases.
    Stitch through the two layers of material all the way round, close to
    the edge of the caste.

14. With the right sides of the two fabrics together, stitch one strip of
    simulated sheepskin along the unbound edge of the boot as shown in Fig. 118.

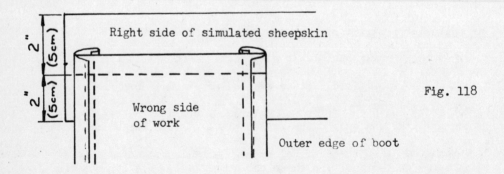

Right side of simulated sheepskin

2" (5cm)

2" (5cm)

Wrong side
of work

Fig. 118

Outer edge of boot

15. Fold the simulated sheepskin up at the stitching line and pin the two
    layers together, to keep them from interfering with the next two steps.

16. Cut a piece of Velcro 8 inches (20 cm.) long.   Separate the two halves
    and stitch one half, with its sticking face up, on to the right side of the
    work, across the boot immediately below the simulated sheepskin.
    Keep the partnering piece of Velcro until Step 22.

17. Using fabric adhesive, stick a strip of foam along the wrong side of the work at the same level as the Velcro, which is on the other side of the work.

18. Cut the elastic in half. (Two pieces each 7 inches long).
Unpin the simulated sheepskin.
Fold in ½ inch (1.25 cm.) along all 4 edges of the simulated sheepskin and tack in place.

19. Place one piece of elastic along the lower half of the free end of the simulated sheepskin. Stitch across each end of the elastic to secure it, stretching it to fit, as shown in Fig. 119.

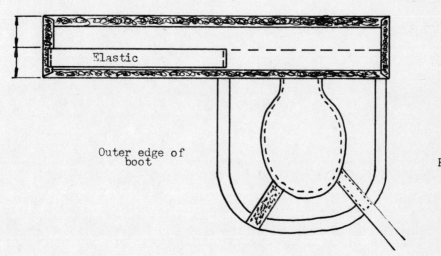

Elastic

Outer edge of boot

Fig. 119

20. Fold the simulated sheepskin in half along its length and stitch it together around the folded in edges.

21. Fold the simulated sheepskin over to the wrong side of the work and stitch it down to enclose the strip of foam. (Fig. 120)

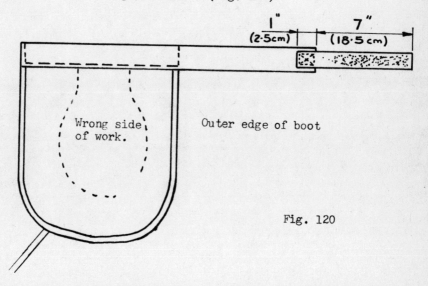

1" (2·5cm)   7" (18·5 cm)

Wrong side of work.

Outer edge of boot

Fig. 120

95

22. With the wrong side of the work uppermost, stitch the piece of Velcro
    left over from Step 16 to the free end of the simulated sheepskin, with
    its sticking face up, as shown in Fig. 120.

Make a second boot to match the first, reversing all pattern pieces and
fastenings.

Each knee boot should be fastened in place with the Velcro strap passing
from the inside to the outside of your horse's leg.

CHAPTER 14

HOCK BOOTS

STYLE A

Note: These boots are made as a pair, so that, when finished, one is a mirror image of the other.

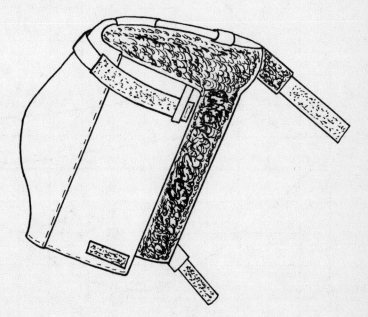

You will need:

4 pieces of simulated sheepskin each 14 inches (36 cm.) x 13 inches (33 cm.)

4 pieces of leatherette (upholstery vinyl) or soft leather each 6 inches (15 cm.) x 13 inches (33 cm.)

4 pieces of blanket-weight material each 7 inches (18 cm.) x 12 inches (30 cm.)

2 strips of ½ inch (1.25 cm.) thick foam each 13 inches (33 cm.) x 1 inch (2.5 cm.)

Fabric adhesive.

31 inches (80 cm.) of 1 inch (2.5 cm.) wide tape.

10 inches (25 cm.) of 1 inch (2.5 cm.) wide strong elastic.

14 inches (36 cm.) of 1½ inch (3.75 cm.) wide Velcro.

To make

For one pair of boots

1. Cut 2 pairs of shape A in simulated sheepskin.   (Save the pieces left over).
   Cut 2 pairs of shape B in leatherette or soft leather.
   Cut 2 pairs of shape C in blanket-weight material.

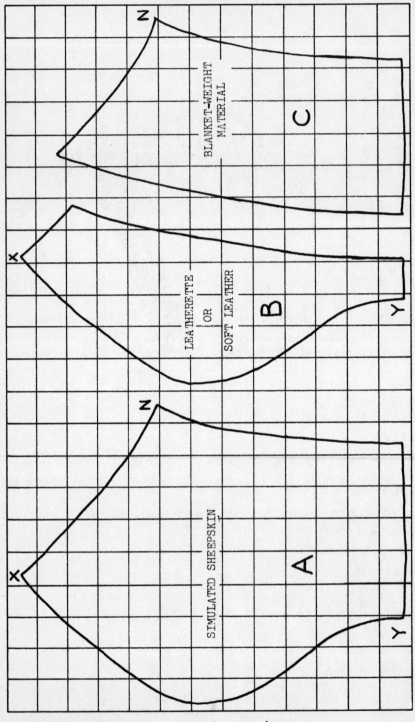

EACH SQUARE REPRESENTS 1 INCH (2.5 CM.)

2. Take one pair each of Shapes A, B and C.
   Join each shape B to each shape C, so that they match shape A which is
   in simulated sheepskin.   Use a flat seam.   (**Fig. 121**)

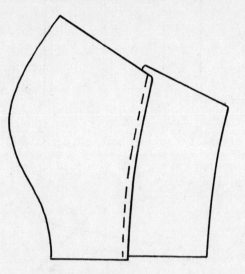

Fig. 121

3. With the right sides of the material together, join 1 pair of shape A
   in simulated sheepskin down seam XY.
   With the right sides of the material together, join one pair of shape B/C
   down seam XY.

4. Cut 3 pieces of tape each 2½ inches (6.5 cm.) long.   Place one piece of tape
   over the centre seam of the simulated sheepskin at the top edge, and one
   piece at each end of the top edge, 1 inch (2.5 cm.) in from the side edge.
   (Fig. 122)

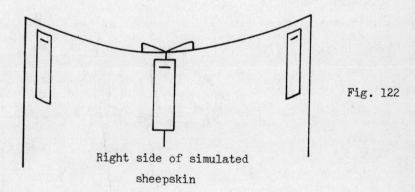

Right side of simulated

sheepskin

Fig. 122

5. With the right sides of the material together, join this pair of shape A
   to the pair of shape B/C along the seam NXN, so that the 3 pieces of tape
   are secured in the seam.   (Fig. 123)

99

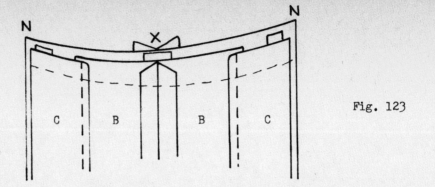

Fig. 123

6. Stick one strip of foam around the top of shape B/C, so that the top edge of the foam is level with the seam stitching, using fabric adhesive. Join both side seams level with the ends of the foam strip. Cut off the top corners of the work.   (Fig. 124)

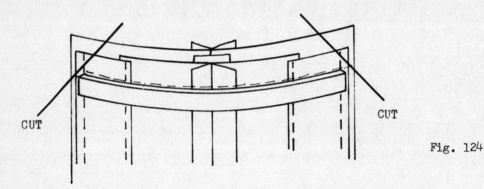

CUT

CUT

Fig. 124

7. Turn the work through to the right side.   Push the top corners into place, using a pair of scissors with the blades closed together.

Leaving the tapes sticking up from the seam, stitch through both layers of material 1 inch (2.5 cm.) down from the top edge, immediately below the foam strip to secure it in place.

Turn ½ inch (1.25 cm.) of the bottom edge of each of the two layers in to the wrong side, and stitch around the lower edge ¼ inch (0.625 cm.) up from the edge.   (Fig. 125)

Fig. 125

8. Fold the three tapes down.   Turn the end ¼ inch (0.625 cm.) of each tape under, and stitch the ends down, using 3 rows of stitching on top of each other.   (Fig. 126)

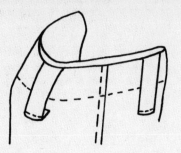

Fig. 126

9. From the pieces of simulated sheepskin left over from cutting out shape A, cut a strip 3 inches (7.5 cm.) x 4 inches (10 cm.).

Fold in ½ inch (1.25 cm.) all the way round.
Fold the strip in half down its length, and stitch around the 3 folded in edges.   (Fig. 127)

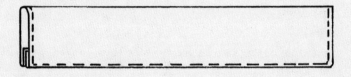

Fig. 127

10. Stitch this strip to the lower inner edge of the boot.
Cut a strip of Velcro 3 inches (7.5 cm.) long, and separate the two halves. Stitch one half, with its sticking face down, to the free end of the strip of simulated sheepskin, and its partner to the lower outer edge of the boot, with its sticking face up, ½ inch (1.25 cm.) in from the side edge of the boot as shown in Fig. 128.

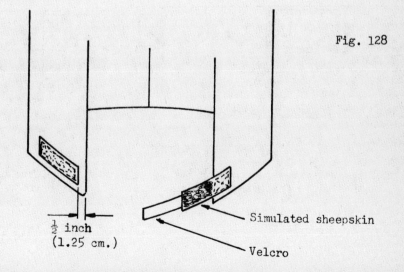

Fig. 128

½ inch
(1.25 cm.)

Simulated sheepskin

Velcro

<u>To make the top strap</u>

11. Cut a piece of simulated sheepskin (from the pieces left over after cutting
out shape A) 7 inches (18 cm.) long x 4 inches (10 cm.) wide.
Cut a piece of tape 8 inches (20 cm.) long.
Cut a piece of elastic 5 inches (12.5 cm.) long.
Cut a piece of Velcro 4 inches (10 cm.) long.

12. Fold in ½ inch (1.25 cm.) all the way round the simulated sheepskin.
Place the elastic along the wrong side of the material at the position
shown in Fig. 129.   Stitch across each end of the elastic to secure it,
stretching it to fit.

Fig.129

13. Fold the simulated sheepskin in half along its length, and stitch around
the folded in edges.

14. Fold the ends of the tape under for neatness.   Stitch one end of the tape
to the simulated sheepskin.
Separate the two halves of Velcro.   Stitch one piece to the tape, and the
other piece on to the simulated sheepskin as shown in Fig. 130.

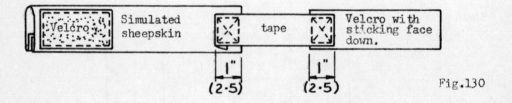

Fig.130

15. Thread this strap through the loops at the top of the hock boot, so that
the Velcro fastening is on the outside of your horse's leg.

Make a second boot to match the first, reversing all pattern pieces and
fastenings.

STYLE B

Note: These boots are made as a pair, so that, when finished, one is a mirror image of the other.

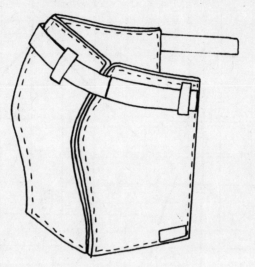

You will need:

4 pieces of blanket-weight material each 22 inches (56 cm.) x 13 inches (33 cm.)

2 pieces of ½ inch (1.25 cm.) thick foam each 22 inches (56 cm.) x 13 inches (33 cm.)

31 inches (80 cm.) of 1 inch (2.5 cm.) wide tape.

10 inches (25 cm.) of 1 inch (2.5 cm.) wide strong elastic.

14 inches (36 cm.) of 1½ inch (3.75 cm.) wide Velcro.

1 piece of simulated sheepskin 14 inches (36 cm.) x 4 inches (10 cm.)

To make

For one pair of boots:

1. In blanket-weight material, cut 2 pairs of shape A and 4 pairs of shape B.
   In ½ inch (1.25 cm.) thick foam, cut 1 pair of shape A and 2 pairs of shape B.

The following instructions are for 1 boot

2. Take one pair of shape A in blanket-weight material and 1 piece of foam. With the wrong sides of the material together, place the piece of foam between the two pieces of blanket-weight material.

3. Take 2 pairs of shape B in blanket-weight material and 1 pair in foam. With the wrong sides of the material together, place a piece of foam between each pair of blanket-weight shapes.

PATTERN 12   —   6 HOCK BOOTS (STYLE B)

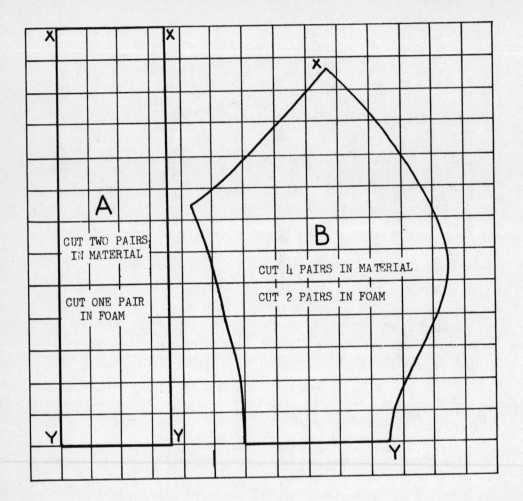

EACH SQUARE REPRESENTS 1 INCH (2.5 CM.)

4. Stitch through all three layers of each shape, close to the edge. Decide which will be the inside surface and which will be the outside of each piece.
   With the inside surfaces together, join 1 shape B to each side of shape A down the seam XY. (Fig. 131)

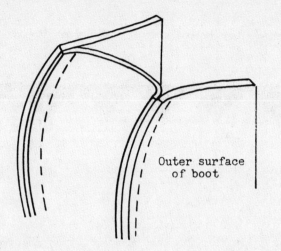

Outer surface
of boot

Fig. 131

5. Trim the seams to within ¼ inch (0.625 cm.) of the stitching line.

6. Cut 3 pieces of tape each 2½ inches (6.5 cm.) long.
   Turn ¼ inch (0.625 cm.) under at each end of the pieces of tape.
   Stitch one piece at the centre top edge and one at each end of the top edge, ½ inch (1.25 cm.) in from the side edge. Use three rows of stitching on top of each other. (Fig. 132)

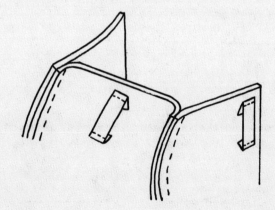

Fig. 132

7. Now follow steps 9 to 14 of Style A Hock Boots.

Make a second boot to match the first, reversing all pattern pieces and fastenings.

CHAPTER 15

COLOURED BROWBAND

You could use velvet, silk or plastic ribbon to cover your browband, although the instructions are for velvet only.   It can be covered in all one colour or in two colours.

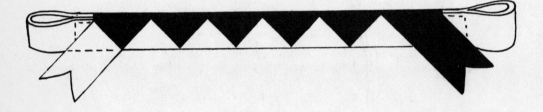

You will need:

A browband (an old one will do, provided the stitching is sound and it is clean).

2 lengths of velvet ribbon the same width as the browband, and each three times its length.

Sewing thread.

To make

1. Place one end of each piece of ribbon together, with the velvet sides outermost, and stitch them together at an angle of 60° about 1 inch (2.5 cm.) from the end.   (Fig. 133)

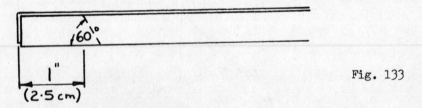

Fig. 133

2. With the outerside of the browband facing you, place the browband between the ribbons as shown in Fig. 134.

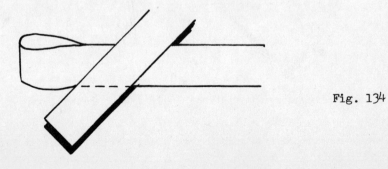

Fig. 134

106

3. Fold the white ribbon over and down between the browband and the black ribbon. (Fig. 135)

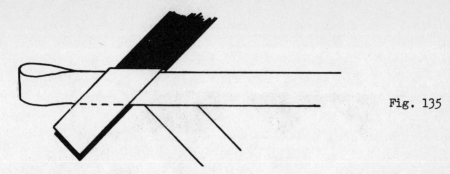

Fig. 135

4. Fold the black ribbon over, down, under and up, so that it covers the white ribbon at the front, and passes between it and the browband at the back. Always finish with the black ribbon pointing upwards. (Fig. 136)

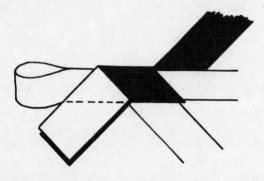

Fig. 136

5. Fold the white ribbon under, up, over and down, so that it covers the black ribbon at the front and passes between it and the browband at the back. Always finish with the white ribbon pointing downwards. (Fig. 137)

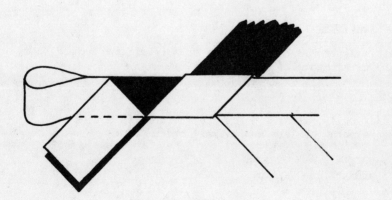

Fig. 137

6. Repeat steps 4 and 5 until the white ribbon reaches the end of the browband.

7. Fold the black ribbon over and down. Stitch the two ends of the ribbon together and cut notches to stop them fraying. (Fig. 138)

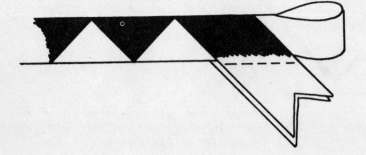

Fig. 138

You may be able to sponge the ribbon clean, but if it gets too dirty, you will have to rebind the browband with fresh ribbon.

SOURCES OF SUPPLY

Straps and buckles

These are often available from retailers specialising in leather craft work or outdoor pursuits.

Fabrics, bindings, etc.

Suitable materials should be obtainable from fabric and haberdashery retailers and departments of large stores.

In case of difficulty, materials for the items in this book are available to personal callers and by mail order from:

B.J. Horsecraft Ltd.,
Baddow Craft and Antique Centre,
The Bringey,
Church Street,
Great Baddow,
Essex.